2

UNITY CENTER
OF EDMONTON
477-5351

Love, Loved, Loving!

JAMES DILLET FREEMAN

Love, Loved, Loving!
The Principal Parts of Life

DOUBLEDAY & COMPANY, INC.   GARDEN CITY, NEW YORK
1974

Library of Congress Cataloging in Publication Data

Freeman, James Dillet.
  Love, loved, loving!

  Poems.
  I. Title.
PS3556.R388L6   811'.5'4
ISBN 0-385-01858-4
Library of Congress Catalog Card Number 73–20511

Contents

VII. If I Do Not Have Love

VIII. Only Love Can Set You Free

IX. They Know Their Own Worth

X. Something in Us Tells Us

XI. Moments of Love

XII. Because I Love You

XVII.   The Miracle of Love

To begin

I sat down to write,
and I asked myself,
"What shall I write?"
My heart said,
"Write about love."
But my mind said,
"Write about wisdom."
My heart did not argue with my mind,
it merely embraced my mind with love.
Then after a while
my mind spoke again and said,
"Love is wisdom."

I. Love Is in Our Genes

WE ARE ALL GOING TO HAVE TO LEARN TO SAY IT

Why do I want to write a book about love?
There have undoubtedly been hundreds of books
written about love.
Love has been discussed from every angle
and even in terms of curves.
It has been the subject of theological treatises
philosophical dialogues
psychological analyses
physiological statistics
biological investigations
anatomical diagrams
artistic masterpieces
pornographic pamphlets
and countless novels, stories, and plays.

I am writing a book about love because
I am in love with love.
I know nothing that I want more,
need more,
or is more important
to my health, happiness, and survival—
and also to yours!
And so I want everybody to learn to
love one another.

I am writing this book to say,
"Love one another."
That is not a very original statement—
though I hope before I am through writing
I will have found some original ways to say it.
"Love one another."
It has been said
by much more important, influential, and loving
people than I.

You can undoubtedly think of a few,
starting with Jesus
and probably ending with your mother,
if you had brothers and sisters.

We all grow weary of hearing it,
but there is a way of saying it
we never get tired of hearing.
For the best way of saying,
"Love one another,"
is to say,
"I love you."
Certainly no one who loved me,
and not even those who didn't,
got tired of hearing that—
they were glad to hear
they were loved!

No matter how often we hear,
"I love you,"
we want to hear it again.
I could toll it like a bell that has one sound,
I could sing it like a bird that has one song,
and you would not tire to hear it
but would hunger yet again
and yet again.

In the final analysis,
it is the way we are all
going to have to learn to say it,
not "You love—one another,"
but "I love—you!"

For only then
will the words become,
not a sermon nobody listens to,
but a lovesong everyone

strains to hear,
and once he hears it
cannot keep
from joining in the chorus.

PUT DOWN THEIR ARMAMENTS AND
REACH OUT THEIR ARMS

Do I think people are going to read my book
and suddenly
start loving one another
and running around saying,
"I love you"?
Do I think they are even suddenly going to
start trusting one another
or not trying to take advantage of one another
or not getting angry with one another?

Do I think the nations
are going to put down their armaments
and reach out their arms
and become one big happy family?

No, I doubt that even many families
are going to become one big happy family.
But on the other hand I know
we are not going to solve our problems
as individuals or nations
until we do love one another.

And we are going to live pitiable half-lives
and deprive ourselves of the rich and beautiful life
we might have
as long as we continue
to cheat and lie and connive against each other
and be unloving,
locked-out inside
where we might find our own inner beauty,
and locked-in outside
where we might be open and free.
We turn ourselves

into miserable misers of spirit,
when we might be lovers and sons of love,
and we turn the earth into an armed camp
where it might be paradise.

WE WANT

There are so many things we want
and feel we have to have—
and things are only a small part
of our problems.
We want to feel important
in our own eyes
and the eyes of others.
We want to stay healthy
and live a long life.
We want to feel safe and secure.
We want to become the very best person
we are capable of being
on every level of being,
physical, mental, and spiritual.
And we want to love
and be loved.

Oh, yes we do.
We want to love and be loved.
We want to love and be loved as much
as we want any or all
of those other things.
Sometimes even more.

We can have the whole world
groveling at our feet
or shouting huzzas in our ears
or piling up riches for us to enjoy—
and if we have no love,
we are creatures starving.

OUR OWN WALLS

Over and over again,
prehistorically,
historically,
and contemporarily,
we human beings
(every civilization,
every culture—
every generation?
every individual?)
have had the same problems to meet.

We come up to the same walls
and we try to get over them
by knocking them down or blowing them up
or finding a secret way around.

But we can't,
because the walls are not where we think they are.
They are not out there
where everybody else is.
They are in us
where we have erected them.
There is no way around them—
they encircle us, not all the others;
they keep us in
more than they keep us out.
Even if we could find a way around other people's walls,
there is no way around our own,
and we cannot blow them up
without blowing ourselves up.

What good are force and conniving
when it is our own walls

and our own self
we have to bring down?

But that's a hard lesson to learn.

IF I HAD TO CHOOSE

If you asked
what power man values
above all his other powers,
most of us would answer,
"His power to think."
But it is interesting
that when we think of someone
as inhuman,
it is not because he is unthinking
but because he is unfeeling.

What makes me less than human
is not my inability to think
but my inability to love.

Man is as much man
because he feels deeply
as because he thinks deeply,
more perhaps.
It is unfortunate for a man
if he is unintelligent,
but it may be unfortunate for all men
if he is heartless.

If I had to choose between intelligence and love,
it would make no difference which I chose.
For if I chose love,
that would show I was intelligent,
and if I chose intelligence,
my intelligence would soon make me loving.

To be intelligent without love
is to be cold;

to be loving without intelligence
is to be sentimental;
to be loving and intelligent
is to be wise.

LOVE IS IN OUR GENES

I don't expect
to suddenly become a saint
and I don't expect
you to.
I don't expect
the nations to suddenly lay down—
like the lion and the lamb together—
all their battleships and missiles and atom bombs.

But human beings have to love one another,
whether they want to or not.
Love is in our genes.
We hunger
the way a miser hungers for his gold
and a sick man hungers for his health
to hear someone say to us,
"I love you."
Oh, yes we do,
whether we know it or not,
whether we admit it or not.
The roughest, the toughest, the most brutal of us—
maybe they more than anybody else,
for the hidden hungers we are afraid to own
gnaw at our vitals
with incessant teeth,
never being satisfied,
where the hunger we face and handle
we occasionally feed.

How lucky we are,
all of us!
That we have learned to use our mouths
more for kissing
than for biting;

for we not only need love as a human individual,
we need love as the human species.
Our survival depends on our becoming
a little less fierce
and a little more friendly.
Let us pray
that the principal explosions we have to deal with
will always be population explosions!

I DON'T SEE A SINGLE TYRANNOSAURUS REX

So these are some of the reasons I've written a book
about love.
I want to say,
"I love you,"
and I want to say,
"Love one another."
And I want to remind myself
and anybody else who chances to read this far
that if it is natural for us to be selfish,
it is also natural for us to love one another.
And we have survived as a species
not because we have been violent
but because we have been able to co-operate.
We are not here after a million years
because we are brutes
but because we have not been brutes.

Through all this million years
the violent have been out
killing off the violent,
and the loving have been staying home
making love,
and as a natural consequence of this
the heirs of the human race
have been getting less violent
and more loving
all the time.

Tyrannosaurus rex and the saber-toothed tiger—
there are a couple of beautiful brutes!
but I don't see a single tyrannosaurus rex or saber-toothed tiger
anywhere
around
any more.

II. What Kind of Love Is Love?

WHAT KIND OF LOVE?

Some of you may be asking,
"What kind of love is this fellow writing about?
Hasn't he read the theologians' learned books
about how many different kinds of love there are?
He sounds as if he thinks the love
a priest feels for his God
is the same as the love
a philanthropist feels for his fellow human beings
and the same as the love
a hero feels for his selfless cause
and the same as the love
a lover feels for his beloved
and the same as the love
a boy feels for his dog
and the same as the love
a blond gold digger feels for her diamonds,
which the songwriters tell us
are her best friends.
He sounds as if he thinks
all love is love."

I know about the theologians' ideas,
though I have not read their books.
Nobody reads the books of theologians
except other theologians
and the students in theological seminaries.
When I began to write, I asked myself,
"What kind of love shall I write about?"
"What kind of love is there?" I wondered.
"I have heard of many kinds," I thought.
"Personal love and impersonal love,
erotic love and selfless love,
human love and divine love.
And there are even those

who when they have used up all the English words they can
    think of
to define and dissect and anatomize love,
turn to Latin and Greek words
so that they can subdivide it even further."

DIFFERENT AND THE SAME

Then I asked myself, "Do you love God?"
"Yes," I said.
"Do you love a beautiful work of art?"
"Yes," I said.
"Do you love your wife?"
"Yes," I said.
"And the feelings you feel as you contemplate your wife or a
    beautiful work of art or God, are they different or the
    same?"
"Different and the same," I said.

The more I thought about that, the more I thought
it was hard to make clear what I thought.
Communication depends on how much we have in common.
Even simple and intellectual concepts
like shoe and hat
or *zapato* and *sombrero*
can be communicated only
if when I make a sound or some marks on a page,
you and I agree
on what the sound and the marks
stand for—otherwise,
when one of us orders a *zapato*
from Sears, Roebuck,
he is likely to end up with his foot
where his head ought to be.
But we need more in common than a language
to communicate any but the easiest ideas.
And love,
though it is even more elemental than a *zapato,*
is harder to communicate—
at least in words.

There are many things we know
and know intensely,
but we cannot convey what we know
to anyone else who does not also know.
The smell of coffee on a morning fire
or how the sun comes out after a rain
or even what sunlight is—
if we try to tell you what these are like we depend,
even more than on our having a common language,
on our having had a common experience.
Most of the things we know
we probably know like this.

AN ELEMENT HAS BEEN ADDED

I remember watching my dog
find out about snow.
I opened the door to let her out
and she stopped in astonishment
and peered and sniffed at the falling flakes
and felt the cold slush under her paws,
and she stood, mistrustful and bewildered,
half in, half out
of a world she suddenly had no acquaintance with.
Then out she leapt,
snapping at the flakes
and dancing and sliding through the slush.
After that she knew what snow is.

Can I tell you what the look in my wife's eyes is like
unless you have looked into your wife's eyes?—
or wished you could?
Can I tell you what I feel when I hear
certain songs or see certain paintings or read certain poems
unless you have music and paintings and poems
that mean as much to you?

Can I tell you what it is like to have a sudden sense
of a Good Presence
where you see no present good,
or to catch a glimpse of heaven's rim when it is hell
unless you, too, have been where I have been
and despaired and sought and found!

What can I say
except that when I love,
something happens between me and what I love;
perhaps the best way to describe it is to say that a door opens—
or is it a wall that is swept away?—

and I see and experience and become something
that was not there before.
An element has been added,
and everything is changed.
Yes, everything.
Not just me.
Not just what I love.
When I love anything,
everything
is heightened and deepened
and takes on meaning
that it did not have before.

Let a wife come into a house
or a beautiful work of art come into the house
or God come into the house
and there isn't a board of the house
that remains the same.

Your wife is just another girl until you love her.
God is just a theological definition until you love him.
A work of art is just a sound of violins
or words on a page
or colors on canvas
until you love it.

Let us consider a work of art.
It is easier to analyze our reaction to a work of art
than it is to our wife or God.
Have you ever thought what happens
when you fall in love with a work of art?

Perhaps you have listened to it or read it or looked at it a
        dozen times
and gone coldly on to something else.
But fall in love with it,
and tears start pouring from your eyes,

26

hot blood starts pumping through your veins,
cold shivers run up and down your back,
and you cannot turn away or put it down.
Perhaps you can never turn away or put it down—
it will be there,
part of your frame of reference,
modifying forever all your view of life.
A love affair with a work of art
can change the very atoms of your universe;
they will shine with a new light,
they will glow with a new life,
and they will dance to a purpose they never had before.

What has happened?
You give your heart to what you love
and it opens its heart to you,
and you step, as it were,
into a new country—
not over a rainbow—
but through the heart—
a world of heightened colors,
sharper feelings,
deeper meaning,
a world where nothing
will ever be the same again
as it was
before you loved.

LET ME NOT OVERLOOK

I try to love God
and I hope he loves me,
but oh, I am grateful
for every morsel of human love that has ever come my way—
after all, it's the only kind
I am capable of myself.

And while I am praising love,
let me not overlook
the love I have shared with my cat and dog—
that has been no mean love
and I am grateful.

I have never loved anyone
or anything
or been loved by anyone or anything
that my life was not deepened by that love.
I was more—
and life was more
because of the love that had been added to it.
The least love gives to life a meaning
all the non-love in the world cannot give it.
The least love is worth more than all the non-love there is.

I have a dog.
Her name is Sharazad-al-jameela.
We call her Zahd.
When my wife and I
got her as a puppy
we had arranged
to take a trip to Hawaii.
I was going to speak there,
so I had to go.

But when Zahd came, my wife said,
"I'm not going."
"But you've never been," I said,
"and you've always wanted to go."
"But now we have a new puppy," she said.
"She is just getting used to us,
learning how to live with us;
I can't leave her now."
She did not go.

At the time I thought,
"This is ridiculous
giving up such a longed-for pleasure trip!"
But the longer I thought about it,
the more clearly I saw
that she was giving up
something unimportant
for something important.

A living creature
is more than a holiday,
and if you have to make a choice
between a pleasure trip
and a love trip,
there is no question
as to the wise choice.

Hawaii was an exciting place
and I enjoyed what I had to do there,
but Zahd is an exciting creature,
and I love her.
Zahd is a whole new dimension
added to life,
so that everything,
including a trip to Hawaii,
has a different meaning

and a different importance
than it had.
Something is present
in our house and in our lives
that was not there before.
She does not always bring us happiness;
sometimes she annoys us,
sometimes she enrages us,
but whatever she brings,
pleasure or pain,
she brings love—
and that's a whole new
window on the world.

The least three-dimension world
has a depth and substance
that the most two-dimension world
does not have.
There is no way to compare them—
they exist on different levels.
That is how it is when love enters a life,
even the least love—
life enters a new dimension
and goes on from there
in a way
totally unlike
whatever it was
before.

GRADING AND DEGRADING LOVE

I love love so much
I don't care to question what kind it is.
You can divide it up as you prefer.
For myself, I am grateful
for all the love that comes my way—
agape and *caritas* and *filia* and *eros*—
I don't care about its nationality
or about its language,
or even if it speaks any language—
some of the best love I have encountered
did not say a word.
I'll take love
personal and impersonal
and human and divine,
any I can get
and any I can give.

I mistrust most of the people who go around
grading and degrading love
and separating it into superior and inferior kinds,
unseen, seen, and obscene!
depending on whether it is attached to
God, humanity, or lovers.

When I hear people prating about
the holy love of God
and the base love of lovers,
they frighten me a little.

Better the basest love
than the most divine indifference!

Which would you prefer—
to be burned by a holy man who "loves" God

or condemned by a righteous judge who "loves" the law
or made "love" to by a sinful prostitute?
Which of these kinds of "love" do you think God
would be most likely
to disapprove of least?

I think we know.
Some holy men and righteous judges once took such a woman
to be judged by love.
Remember the story?*
In the story,
when love looked up from having written its judgment in the
        sand—
and is that not where love would write judgments,
where they might be wiped away
by any passing wind or rain?—
when love looked up, I say,
and gazed around,
you know which ones had slunk away.
I can still hear the voice of love
saying to the woman,
the only one who dared remain
when love lifted its eyes
and turned its penetrating gaze upon the soul,
"Neither do I condemn you; go and sin no more."

Loving God
is sometimes an excuse
for not loving human beings.

* I note in the Revised Standard Version of the Bible
  they have taken this story out of the text
  and put it in small type in the footnotes.
  It is an interesting commentary on the theological mind
  that of all the stories in the Bible—
  and have you ever read all of them?—
  this lovely story of love
  is the only one
  they have taken out.

Don't misunderstand me.
I'm not writing a book
in praise of prostitutes.
I grew up in the middle of a red-light district;
prostitutes were my friends;
and I never knew a "happy hooker"—
though I knew a number who were alcoholics
and several who committed suicide
or tried to.

Prostitutes and priests,
both are capable of
selfish and unselfish acts.

THEY STAYED FAITHFUL TO HUMANITY

This is a book in praise of love,
whatever form it may take,
and in praise of lovers,
whatever else they may have been.
For the most part, though religion may have produced some
        rigid, narrow, condemning people,
there is no doubt that it has also produced more loving, gentle,
        self-denying people
than any other human activity.
I don't know whether it is because
it is hard to have faith in God
and not love human beings,
or it is hard to love human beings
and not have faith in God.
At any rate, the history of religion
is almost the history of selfless people
who have given all they had,
even their life,
to relieve human suffering—
people like Saint Francis
or Saint Teresa
or Father Damien.

When the Nazis began to persecute the Jews,
Einstein said he expected his intellectual friends
to rise up in protest,
the philosophers, the writers, the scientists, the artists, the college
        professors—
they were the bold freethinkers and lovers of truth.
But when they saw the concentration camps
and the gas chambers,
their boldness evaporated
and hardly a murmur rose from their ranks.
The men who stood up
and denounced the Nazi horrors,

even at the cost of having to endure them,
were little unknown parish priests and country preachers,
for whom intellectuals like him had had only contempt
and from whom he expected nothing.
They stayed faithful to humanity—
lest they might be false to God?

We have probably all known a few such people.
I have known one or two
who, on a bitter winter day,
meeting someone who had no coat,
would take off their own coat
and wrap him in it—
I take off my hat to them.

Recently I read about the beatification of
Maximilian Maria Kolbe,
a Franciscan friar.
When ten prisoners
in the concentration camp at Auschwitz
were chosen to be starved to death as punishment
because a prisoner who had escaped had not been recaptured,
Father Kolbe stepped forward
and asked if he could take the place of one of them
who had a family.
In the death cell
he was the last to die,
encouraging the others
as long as they were alive.
I am deeply moved
by Father Kolbe's love.

But also I have been deeply moved
by the stories I have read of love
that lovers have had for their lovers
and mothers have had for their children
and friends have had for one another.

POSSIBILITY OF PARADISE

I admire great and selfless men
like Albert Schweitzer and Father Damien,
but I have never felt that it is necessary
to go live in a jungle
or in a leper colony
in order to show how much we love
God or man.
If it takes that to improve the world,
it is going to be a long time
before the world gets much improvement.
I have always wondered about the people who go off
to the ends of the earth
to be spiritual.
The worst jungles I know about
are not in Africa.
Missionaries to Africa
are in the same fix as the preacher
who delivered a sermon on the benefits of giving.
"It is the duty of the rich," he said,
"to give to the poor."
A friend asked him if he thought he had
convinced anybody.
"Oh yes," he said, "I convinced the poor."

But those who have gone off into the slums
and the jungles
have not convinced the poor
any more than the rich,
at least not the poor I've known.
The difference between rich and poor
is not a difference in selfishness.
If anything, the rich
are less selfish than the poor—
they are just not enough less selfish.

If I were going to be a missionary,
I think I could do more good for the world
in New York City or Miami Beach or Washington
than in a jungle—
and I don't mean in the slums of those cities.
If I could just convince a few millionaires
that Mammon was not a jealous god,
they could worship the God who is love, too!
or convince a few world statesmen
that they would be better off
not being cannibals,
think of all the good I would do!

I would not have to change them much—
a little love makes so great a difference.
I would not even want to change them much—
too much change might not be good
for them
or us.
When the good Buddhist king Asoka
gave up his throne to become a monk,
he set his world back, not forward.
They would have to be
such a little bit less selfish than they are.

I don't mean share the wealth.
Down through history
sharing the wealth
usually has turned out to be
sharing the poverty.
Giving money
does not make people rich.
What makes people rich
is making money.
I don't want the rich and powerful and able
to stop being rich and powerful and able
and become saints in sackcloth and solitary.

The rich and powerful and able
make first-rate motor magnates
and oil company presidents
and world leaders,
and they probably would not be worth the leather
it would take to keep them in sandals
as Trappist monks
or even abbots.
But if they would just keep on building cars
or pumping oil
or being president or governor,
only doing it more for the general good
rather than their own,
what a different world we would have then!

We talk a lot about the possibility of paradise—
do you know how far away it is?
No further than a few small acts of love.

WHAT HAND DID YOU EXPECT HIM TO USE?

Love is not something
showered down on us like rain
out of the heavens.
The only love I have ever run into
has always begun in someone's human heart.

If I cannot love those whom it is easy to love—
my wife, my mother, my sister, my child—
how will I love those it is hard to love?
If I don't love what it is natural to love,
will I love what is supernatural?
God himself has told us that those who say
they love God whom they have not seen
and do not love those close and dear to them
whom they have seen—
they are liars.
The love that is God is first of all
the love that is human.

A woman in desperate need
went into a church to pray.
She cried out,
"God, if there is a God,
let me become aware of your presence.
I need to feel you as
a real loving help in my life."
Just then she felt a hand brush her shoulder.
She burst into tears of joy and sprang up.
When she turned around, a friend
was standing behind her.
"I was praying to God
to come to me," she said,
"and I thought I felt his hand,
but it was yours, wasn't it?"

Her friend looked at her gently for a moment.
"What hand did you expect him to use?" she said,
"but the hand that was closest to you!"

If God is love,
must it not be true
that human love is divine
and divine love is human?
If God is love,
is there any love that is not divine?

I LIKE THAT LITTLE MONK

I have always liked
the little barefoot monk who went around in a coarse robe
doing good.
He was such a good man
and worked so hard to help people
and to lessen their pain
that even God was impressed
and sent his angel down to him.
"You have been so loving
God has sent me to reward you," said the angel.
"You may have any blessing your heart desires."
"But I already have everything I desire,"
said the monk.
"Oh, now, there must be something," insisted
the angel. "Ask for anything. You may have it."
The monk thought for a long while.
At last he said,
"In that case, wherever I pass,
as my shadow falls behind me,
let whatever it falls on
be blessed."

I like that little monk—
I think he understood the true worth of things
and the source of true happiness.

But I like my wife no less—
she rises early in the morning
to cook the breakfast she knows I like
even though she herself does not eat breakfast.

And I like myself sometimes
when I have the power to injure someone I don't like
and I refrain from injuring him.

Love
for the most part
is made up not of glorious and selfless
acts of martyrdom,
but of little thoughtfulnesses,
kindnesses,
courtesies.
Sometimes it is just
smiling
or opening a door
or writing a letter.
Sometimes it is
even less than that—
it is just not doing
an unkind act you might have done.

MOMENTS OF MERCY

Men may have moments of mercy,
only moments perhaps,
but precious moments!
Once in a while,
my foot pauses as it descends
lest it crush the ant;
I capture the wasp
and carry it out of the room
rather than destroy it;
I don't like starlings,
they seem like bullies
and crowd out birds I do like
but they have flown down my chimney
into the fireplace,
and once or twice I've risked life and house
to pluck them out of the flames
and carry them out into the open air again.
As for human beings,
I have occasionally been kind
to those who have injured me.

Soldiers about to kill an enemy
who had been trying to take their life
have been known to withhold the blow,
so I have heard.

I wonder if any other species of creature
has moments of mercy.
I wonder if the starling ever pauses
with its sharp beak above a worm
because it feels compassion for it,
or the wasp ever feels pity
for the caterpillar and withholds its sting,

or the ant about to devour an enemy
suddenly turns away
because it decided it does not want to kill.
I have a dog and I used to have a cat,
both intelligent
and sensitive animals;
but I have never seen either of them
forbear its fierce pursuit
of some little creature
because it suddenly was moved
with pity.

We may have only moments of mercy—
only moments!—
but what a long climb we have made
to come that far.

III. Of Rabbits and Buddhas

IS LOVE GOD?

"The Bible may say God is love,"
said the preacher,
"but it does not say love is God."
I considered what the preacher said.
By the laws of logic, I decided, he may be right.
Just because A is B, it does not follow
that B is necessarily A.
I doubt, however, that the laws of logic
present the whole picture
where God is concerned,
even though he set them up for us human beings
to measure truths by—
they especially don't count for much
where love is concerned.

Then I tried to think of all the different
aspects of love that I could think of.
Try as I would, I could not think of one
that was not beautiful and good,
and was not worthy of being thought of as divine,
if you wanted to use that word.
I recalled that the same book in the Bible
that says God is love,
also makes the point that we are
prone to separate
love connected with God from love
connected with human beings,
but the only kind of love connected with God that
can count as love
is the love that includes human beings.
You're kidding yourself, the book says,
if you say you love God
and your love is not connected
with human beings.

47

If your love does not include
the living things
you see and live with,
it does not include God,
whether you say it does or not.
And if your love does take in living things,
it includes God,
whether you know it does or not.

I have watched a fledgling blackbird fly into
the branches of a tree and become lodged there
by its fright,
afraid to try the air again,
and I have seen how for days its father and mother
have brought it food and hovered near to protect it.
That has seemed a very high order of
love to me.
I wonder what kind of love the preacher has in mind
when he tells me that although God is love,
love is not God.
It has to be a lower kind of love
than that of blackbirds.

IMAGINE IMAGINING HELL

While we are on the subject of God as love,
perhaps we should have a word about
God as the inventor of hell.

Whoever made up hell
was not much of a lover.
That's why I know it wasn't God.
God is love.

Whoever invented hell
must not have liked people
or God.

Imagine imagining hell—
aren't you glad you didn't?
What a misery-pit of a mind
such a thought had to come out of!

What a loathing for your fellow human beings you would have
   to feel
to believe them worthy of eternal damnation—
yes, even the worst of them!
and what a low opinion of the Maker of the world you would
   have to have
to believe he would be mean enough to make such a dungeon
in which to torture the people he himself made
the way he made them!
To believe that, you would have to believe
in a God even meaner than you.

I remember reading of a Christian missionary and a Buddhist
   monk
who were discussing their religion.
"We believe in hell," said the Christian.

"We believe in seven hells," said the Buddhist.
"Ah yes, so you do," said the Christian,
"but we believe in a God who will see that you get there."

If you can have such a wicked thought
as to believe God would invent such a wickedness as hell,
there is no limit to the wickedness
you may attribute to him.
Some people have imagined him sending people to hell
for love!
That's the supreme contradiction—
Love damning lovers!
Usually for loving a person
who was not on the damners' approved list,
or loving in a way
that was not on the damners' approved list,
or just for loving too much.
Dante, who made hell popular,
populated whole sections of his hell
with lovers.

Most of us have been in hell at times,
not the kind the preachers threaten us with,
but hell enough—
but we are not there because we love too much,
only because we love too little.

A FEW SAINTS AND SINNERS

Pretty obviously
nobody
or almost nobody
has ever lived
altogether by love.
We don't know how.
Could we even eat?
We have to kill to eat,
and that hardly seems an act of love.
I believe the ox and the radish,
if they were polled, would object
to our being included among
the altogether loving.

I suppose there are a few foods—
some of the fruits—that give themselves to be eaten.
They want you to carry them away
so that their seeds will be scattered.

There are stories about a few saints and saviors
altogether loving—
but they are mostly stories.

When the Buddha was on the way to becoming the Buddha,
he was once a rabbit,
I have read.
As a rabbit he came upon a poor beggar starving to death.
He immediately decided he would save the beggar's life
by leaping into the fire
and making the beggar a gift of himself
in the form of roast rabbit.
But before he did this,
he paused and shook himself
and informed the fleas who were feasting on him

51

of what he was about to do
so that they would not have to endure his sacrificial pyre
unless they had a mind to.
I have always thought that while this
might be thought of as exemplary behavior for a Buddha,
it was peculiar behavior for a rabbit.
If I were a rabbit I would abjure this rabbit-buddha
as unrabbitly
and a disgrace to the species.
Jesus was not always so willing
to bestow a sacrificial blessing
on anybody or anything.
He overturned the money-changers' tables
and whipped them out of the Temple courtyard;
he blasted the fig tree
whose conduct fell short
of what is to be expected of fig trees—
I wonder what he would have thought
of such an unrabbitly rabbit!—
he had some harsh epithets
for a number of people
whose behavior he did not approve of.

There is a story in the Pseudepigrapha
(the books that did not get into the Bible)
about the Apostle John.
He came one night to an inn
infested with bedbugs.
He blessed them and obediently and happily
they all trailed out into the night
and let him sleep.
The next morning when he left
they all trailed back in again
to wait for a less saintly traveler.

I have wondered if a saint

might not have been better able to share a little of his blood with
    those bedbugs
than the unfortunate fellow
who came to bed the next night after John.
Those bedbugs must have been ravenous by then!

There is an ascetic Hindu sect
called the Jains.
They are the most self-denying people on earth
(and probably have more rich bankers than any other group in
    India.)
Some Jain holy men go along the streets
carrying mattresses swarming with bedbugs.
Jain householders throw them coins,
whereupon they lie down on their mattress
and let the bedbugs bite them.
That way everyone has a spiritual feast—
the hungry bedbug,
the ascetic holy man,
and the charitable householder.

PERFECT LOVE

I have not come to the place where I can live by perfect love,
I don't know how.
And I don't believe I am expected to.
If I were expected to, I believe
I would know how.
In order to live,
I have to eat
and in order to eat
I have to kill.
In a world where I lived by love,
I would not have to do that.
But since I do,
it must be acceptable to life—
so let it be acceptable in my eyes.
I have to love where I can
and be as reverent toward life as I am able,
and when I have to dig up a potato
or bake wheat into bread
or slaughter an ox,
I have to do it knowing
that at the level I have come up to,
this is the way it has to be.
I don't know how to live on water and air
or turn clods of earth into living cells
the way a plant does.
But I don't think
algae that live without taking life
serve life any more than I.
Algae merely have to be what algae are,
but I become what I am
by refusing to be less
and making a struggle
to be more than I might have been.

The algae and the plankton are what they are.
I bless them and rejoice in their being.
But I have a sense that I am love's child
no less than the algae and the plankton;
and perhaps I am even dearer to love,
because I have to desire to love,
and aspire to love,
and learn to love.
I have to love love so much
I try to love
even when it's hard.

I have to affirm that this is love's world
even when I don't see how it can be;
I have to try to love
when it would be easier
and even seem more reasonable
not to.
Even when I see all sorts of reasons
for believing this is not love's world,
I can still rise up out of the welter
of pain and strife and selfishness
and perform some selfless act,
not to gain advantage,
but just to be loving,
just because I believe
that in spite of all appearances to the contrary,
that is the way I was meant to be.
And even if the world was not made this way
and there is nothing in the nature of things
that decrees that I have to love,
then I still say,
"That is the way it ought to be."
And whether there is a single atom in the whole universe
that cares whether I love or not,
I care whether I love or not
and I care whether it is loved;

and I shall try to love
and make the world a world of love
as far as I am able,
because I know that is the way the world ought to be
and the only way it can be
and be a world worth being in.

SOMEWHERE BETWEEN THE
RABBIT AND THE BUDDHA

Somehow it is impossible
for me to believe
that love
has to result
in denial,
sacrifice,
and asceticism.
If the end result of love
is always sacrifice and suffering,
we must be on the wrong path—
and the whole world must have a gigantic flaw at its center.
If Love made us and the world,
I cannot believe it made us to suffer.
With what limited love I am capable of feeling,
I don't want those I love to suffer—
that's the last thing I want.
I don't even want those I don't love to suffer—
not very often anyway.
I have to get very angry with them
to wish them misfortune
and then very shortly
I'm ashamed of myself
for wishing such a wish.

Somehow I do not believe
life has made me
in order to provide a feast for bedbugs
or to be a hungry beggar.

There is something in my nature
that finds something repugnant to the whole way of things
about a rabbit that leaps into a fire,
or a man who lets bedbugs devour him,

or wears a mask
so that he will not accidentally
swallow a gnat.

If the bagworms destroy my evergreens
and the aphids ruin my roses
and the rabbits eat my beans and beets to the ground,
then I have to choose
between bagworms, aphids, and rabbits
and evergreens, roses, and food.

Have I any choice
as a man
except to dispose of the pests
as humanely
and efficiently
as possible?

Perhaps the day will come
when I will know how to permit
bagworms and evergreens both to flourish,
but the bagworms I have known will eat the evergreens to the
        last green needle if I let them.

I have heard that Albert Schweitzer
would treat children in his Lambaréné hospital,
while poisonous spiders hung from webs
in his clinic.
But for all his reverence for life,
I observe that he drew the line
when it came to the bacteria causing his patients to be ill;
he destroyed them by every means at his disposal,
perhaps with a prayer for their soul first,
I don't know about that.

Many primitive people,
before they harvest their crops,

offer a sacrifice to the ancestors
of the wheat and rice
they are about to take for their food.
I like that,
as I like giving grace before a meal—
it puts things in their right perspective.

Perhaps, this is what is needed most of all—
to put things in their right perspective,
to draw the line at the right point.

I am meant to live lovingly
but I am meant to live.
At the present moment of my unfoldment,
I do not know how to live
without some unloving acts.
Therefore it cannot be unacceptably unloving
for me to take life that I need to take
in order to live.
But I have to consider every such act
in the light of the effect.

I remember Gandhi's saying
he would starve
before he would eat meat.
And for him that was the right action to take,
I am sure.
But it would not be the right action for most
persons to take,
and I am sure he would have been the loudest in declaring that
        that is so.

There were many unsuccessful attempts to assassinate him,
before someone finally succeeded.
Gandhi, of course, never resisted any of them.
After one such attempt, his son asked him,
"Father, if I had been there,

I would have tried to keep the assassin
from killing you—
would that have been wrong?"
"My son," said Gandhi,
"it would have been just as wrong
for you not to have resisted him
as it would have been for me
to resist."

The Mahatma was a very wise man.
He knew that all of us are at all levels of unfoldment,
and each of us has to live at the level
he has come up to.
Life asks us to be true to our own truth,
and it asks us to be loving.
To be loving may mean
that the Buddha should freely offer himself to be killed
so that someone else may live,
but it does not mean that a rabbit should.
Most of us are somewhere between
the rabbit and the Buddha,
and what life asks of us is that we be
what we are capable of being.
That it demands—
and make no mistake,
when we fail to meet the demand,
we pay the most dreadful punishment life ever exacts:
we might have been more
and we were not.

I HAVE TO MAKE CHOICES

God,
why did you have to make me
so that I have to play god—
I'm not a very good one.
You have given me the power of life and death
over so many things,
sometimes even over other people.
The way you've made me
and the world I find myself in,
I don't have any choice—
I have to make choices.

But who am I to say
that squashes
are to be preferred to
squash bugs,
or roses to aphids,
or dogs to fleas!

As far as I can tell,
looking around me
and seeing how things are
and what comes natural to me,
you have made me
to be a gardener
in a world you made
to be a wilderness.
You have made me to hate weeds
in a world that seems
to have been especially designed
for weeds to flourish in.
And I don't have any choice—
I have to uproot the weeds
or I play false to the corn and roses

that depend on me to grow,
and to something deep in my own nature,
and to my fellow human beings
who look to my garden for food,
and even to you!

God, I think you meant me to love—
but it is very hard to be a gardener
and love weeds
or a doctor
and love germs
or an engineer
and love the wilderness—
or to be almost anything a human being
seems meant to be
and not have something
it's up to me to eliminate!

I have to see things then
in the order of their importance.
Perhaps I ought to put you first,
but it seems to me the best way to do that
is to put myself and my fellow human beings
at the top of the list to be preferred
above everything else—
then I can work down from there,
preferring whatever
brings joy and health and long life and freedom from fear and
       the development of the mind and mutual love and a better
       human community,
and doing whatever I can or must
to see to it that these human goods
are taken care of and advanced,
and to eliminate all that keeps them
from coming forth.
When I do that,
I believe that's about as loving

as can be expected of me.
Since I have to play god,
let it always be
to help everyone
including myself
to be more truly human.

IV. In a World Love Made

IN A WORLD LOVE MADE

If God is,
he has to be love.
He may be more,
infinitely more,
but nothing less.
For him to be less
would be a contradiction in terms;
he would have to be false
to his own godliness.
For if he is God,
he cannot be less than perfect.
And if he is not loving,
think then what he must be!
Can you believe the Perfect One
is that?

Sometimes God,
the way some of his worshipers describe him to me,
seems more like a demon
than like God.
Such a god might fill a world with pain.
But when I hear about a mean god,
I do not believe in him—
I just think it means
he has mean worshipers.

If God is,
then God is love,
and if God is love,
then it is love that made this world
with all this pain in it.
I have asked all my life:
How did love ever come to make a world like this?

I wonder if there has ever been a thinking human being who
    hasn't asked it—
haven't you?

One thing has to be—
the pain has to be necessary,
not to God
but to me.
And when I do not need the pain,
when I reach the place where I live by love
instead of by pain,
the pain will last no longer—
this I have to believe,
to believe in a world love made,
and I have to believe that.

This pain has to be helping me to become
something more,
something I cannot see
but something I deeply desire,
something of utmost worth,
something worth the pain!
though sometimes I certainly wish
there had been another way
of growing to be
whatever I am growing to be.

Some people apologize for God. They say,
"It's the best world he knew how to make."
But if God is, he is intelligence
as much as he is love—
perfect intelligence and perfect love!
It's not enough to say,
he didn't know how.

No, if this world was made by God,
it has to be perfect.

But when you and I look, we see
all kinds of imperfections.
Then it must mean
that we're not looking right
and there's a lot more to it
than you and I are seeing,
and a way of looking at it
we don't know how to look.

Because the way it looks to me
sometimes
it looks like one helluva world—
and feels like one, too.
I write this with a headache.
I have asked myself this all my life
and tried to figure it out
on some kind of logical basis,
because I am logical—
he made me that way!—
and I believe—
yes, in spite of all my questions, I believe
that this is a world
made by God—
and by God I mean
perfect love and intelligence.

I know—
the scientist fellows have taught me this
even more than the religious fellows—
that the world is not what it seems to be,
that it is made up of invisible particles
that are more waves than anything else—
sheer shimmering light and nothing more.
I live in an electric sea;
this solid ground, this transparent air,
they are only the momentary shape of motion,

rivers of fire, too light for me to see,
who am myself
this dazzling, dancing, electric radiance!

I like this world that science believes in.
It's a world beautiful and perfect enough
for a god who is love and intelligence
to have made it,
and it is a world
obviously capable of becoming
whatever we make it to be.
Since it is light,
pure perfect light,
the way it happens
depends on how I see it—
I don't mean with my eyes
but with my whole way of seeing.

At least this takes the onus
for it's being what it seems
off God,
and puts it on me.
It's my world,
the kind I might have made—
I can believe that.

My eyes respond to a narrow band of light;
my senses report what they report;
my thoughts arrange the world by their synaptic equations;
I funnel God's world
through my mind and body,
and it comes out looking like
what it looks like.
God's river of light
is an infinite river;
I scoop it up in the cup of me,
and the shape it has

in my little vessel,
that's all the infinite can be.
The infinite is like water
and takes the shape of any container—
and the container in which I catch
the infinite
is me.

Have you ever taken one of those ink-blot tests?
You look at some black smudges
and you make out what is there.
The world I think
is much like that.
Except that God didn't use ink blots.

In the beginning . . . he said,
"Let there be light,"
and he poured out light,
living, dancing light,
rainbow rivers of light,
and he said,
"You make it what it is to be."

WHAT OTHER WORLD COULD I BE IN?

As I say,
I have struggled all my life
with this question of a world with so much pain in it,
and the best explanation I have come up with
as to how God could have made it
is that it is the world for me.
It is the world the way it has to be to have me in it.
Could love and intelligence make a better world than that—
for me?

What kind of world could love make
except the one that is best for me
and you
and everything else
that love has made?
Is this not such a world as I need,
the me I have come to be,
with my present limitations, frustrations,
hallucinations, sensations, cerebrations,
disputations, deifications, temptations,
transmigrations, materializations, permutations,
predations, re-creations, expectations,
fabrications, flagellations, individualizations,
and etceteras.
Am I not exactly such a creature
as is made for this world
and this world is made for?

This is a living world,
a world that changes and grows
as I change and grow,
and so it is always the world that is right for me
and for everything else in it.

It is not this or that
or any one thing
to all of us
who have to make it their world.
It is the infinite creation
of an infinite creator,
and so it is
what it has to be
to be the right and fitting habitation
of everything that lives in it.
It has an infinite power of accommodation,
and so it is a brutal world for brutes,
a hellish world for demons,
a heavenly world for angels,
and a human world for human beings,
which means that it has to be
imperfect enough to allow for our imperfections
and perfect enough to allow for our becoming that.

This cannot be a world of perfect bliss,
much as I think I would like it to be,
for I am in it,
and I feel pain and fear and doubt and anger.
In a perfect world
where there were only beings that had perfected themselves,
there would be no place for me.
And I could never find myself
in a world of perfect evil,
for I am capable of love and hope and faith.
What other world could I be in
and still be me,
except this world of depths and heights,
of hopes and hungers,
of peace and passion,
of fear and faith,
of joy and pain—
this sometime world

for this sometime thing—
a world
where world and I may be less
than I would have us become
but where we may become
more than we were!

I look around and see
that it is a world for other creatures
much like myself—
different only in degree,
whether they be blades of grass, ants, magpies, or starfish.
Each one can be itself,
whatever it has come up to being,
though I am not sure that a starfish
is a starfish to a starfish
or even that a starfish is—.

THE I I SEE

I can only be sure
that I am myself
to me—
or can I be sure of that?
Do I have more than the merest surface view of me
and see myself in my mind as in a mirror,
which gives only a one-sided
and dimensionless
reflection of—what?

What do I look like,
to myself or you?
Is this the me that I was made to be
when love said, "Let there be . . ." and there I was?
Do we even all agree
as to the me we are seeing?
You who read my book have your me.
The friends of my youth have their me.
The people I work with have their me.
My mother had her me—I have a feeling
we always look like small boys to our mother.
My son has his me—once or twice he has made me unhappy
when he angrily told me what I looked like to him—
thank God that's not the way he sees me all the time!
My grandson has his me—I believe
my grandson's me would be a delightful fellow to be acquainted
    with.
My wife has her me—I am sure I am to her
a different person than anyone else sees;
for her sake I had better be!
What then do I really look like?

A Japanese girl became my friend.
When she went back to Japan,

she left me a gift—
she had painted my portrait.
But in the portrait I am
Japanese!
I was very flattered, but
I don't look Japanese to me.

For that matter, do not even snapshots indicate
that the I I see
is not a certain, fixed, definite thing
but only the changing impression
I make at any moment?
A scientific instrument like a camera—
that ought to see what is there.
But how different one photograph is
from another!

Is it possible
that everybody's view of me,
including my own,
is only the fleeting picture
snapped from one viewpoint
at one moment,
and the real I of me
is something else?
The Hindus believe that.
They like to talk about the Self
with capital letters,
which is the way God made me,
the perfect creation
of perfect love and intelligence;
and the lower case self
which is the way you or I
happen momentarily to catch sight of me.

This real Self—
can we ever see that?

I think we can.
But we have to want to a great deal,
or we will settle for our usual view—
we'll stop at face and limbs
or at least get no further
than the impression of personality.
I usually think of myself
as mind and body,
but once in a while
I get a hint of more than that.
I wonder if mind and body
are not a divinely clever
walkie-talkie
I use to get around in
and communicate with others.

As I say, to see the real Self
something has to make us look beyond this—
and we have to look with eyes of love.

We have to look with eyes of love,
and then we see
whatever we look at
the way love made it to be.

That is why lovers gaze enrapt
at what they love;
they see it as it is
the way love made it to be,
and so they see
a perfect creation—
would love make anything else?

Have you never thought it strange that what you love
is always beautiful?
We ask you what you see
and you have no words to tell us.

You have looked past the limited forms
that words are able to describe,
and caught a glimpse of a beauty we do not see
and a perfection we only hope at.

We look at what you see
in the imperfect way we look at everything,
and we shrug and turn away, thinking,
"The fellow must be mad to think
he sees such beauty here."

But oh, what I would give
for more of this love madness—
to see what the potter sees
where I see only mud,
to see what the sculptor sees
in the obdurate shapeless stone,
to see what the lover sees
gazing at his beloved.

It is not because the lover sees what is not,
but because he sees what is,
that he cries out, "Beautiful!"
It is we who do not look with eyes of love
who miss the beauty that is truth
and the truth that is always beauty.

Love sees the facts and flaws
but knows that they are not reality.
Love knows the imperfections of others,
yet sees them perfect.
For when we look with eyes of love,
we see what is there
the way it would look
if we could see it
the way love made it to be.

PAST THE SEEMING AND THE SURFACE

I wonder if everyone does not have a sense
of a higher reality
than the reality he ordinarily
has access to.
I wonder if everyone does not have moments
when the veil—for a moment—
separates—or is thinned at least—
and he sees through to a reality more real
than the real world of every day—
he sees through to perfection's imminence.

Nothing changes things
more than love does.
When we love,
nothing looks the same
as it did before.
Everything is heightened,
everything is deepened,
everything becomes more beautiful.

I think that heaven
is our view of things as they look
when we look at them
with eyes of love.
To look with eyes of love—
that's enough, isn't it,
to make us fit for heaven
and to make everything
look heavenly!

That's how Jesus performed his miracles:
he looked with eyes of love.
He didn't see men sick.

He saw them whole;
for he saw them the way they have to be
if love made them—
could love make less than wholeness?
He didn't see two fish and a few stale loaves;
he saw the abundant provision
that love had made for those it loved—
isn't that what you would see
if you saw with eyes of love—
isn't that how the world made by love must look!
And take his disciples,
what a rowdy, ignorant, fearful, ordinary lot they were
until he turned his eyes of love on them,
and then he saw
not frightened fishermen
and foolish farmers,
but the beautiful children of love
that love had made them to be—
and the sick became whole, and the hungry were fed,
and his little bumbling band of uncertain disciples
became the strong men of God love had made them to be
and changed the whole world's way
of looking at itself—
yes, there is none of us
who is not a little more likely
to look at things from love's viewpoint—
at least a little more—
than he would have
had it not been for this man
looking at us all with eyes of love!

I remember reading somewhere
someone's clever
definition of a friend
as someone who knows us
and still likes us.

But another man put the case
the way it really is.
A famous man—I've forgotten who—
was known for his ardent
and violently expressed dislike
of another famous man.
When a friend said,
"Let me introduce him to you,"
he said, "No,
if I knew him,
I'd undoubtedly like him—
and that I don't want to do."

I have never gotten to know anyone well
that I did not like him,
and the better I have gotten to know him
the better I have liked him.
I have known a few people well who were
miserably mean,
even to me,
and I didn't like what they did to people,
but I loved them
because I had gotten to know them well enough
that I had gotten through the ugly wall they raised
and found a beautiful human being.
Getting to know such persons
has convinced me
that if we could get to know anyone
well enough,
get beyond the obvious personality,
no matter how unpleasant that might seem
or his actions might be,
we would find a beautiful person.

But the only way we ever reach
past the seeming and the surface
is through love.

V.　Love, Loved, Loving

LOVE, LOVED, LOVING

Some people are afraid of love
because they are afraid that love will bring them
suffering.
When you love,
you identify yourself with what you love,
and so you endure
its losses and its pains.
If you love,
does it not mean
that you will suffer more
than if you do not love?

This is what the Buddha told the grandmother
who came to him weeping because her grandson had died.
"Would you like to have as many grandsons
as there are people in the city?"
he asked her.
She said she would.
"Then you would have nothing but sorrow," he said.
"For people die in the city every day.
If you have a hundred loved ones,
you have a hundred griefs.
If you have ten loved ones,
you have ten griefs.
If you have one loved one,
you have one grief.
And if you have no loved ones,
you have no griefs."

But I like the story Boys Town tells
about the boy who came one snowy night
carrying another boy on his back,
stumbling and sweating under the weight.
When Father Flanagan (founder of Boys Town) said to him,

"That's a heavy load for you,"
the boy replied,
"He ain't heavy, Father.
He's my brother."

The boy had a wisdom
the Buddha had not learned.

It is hard to understand this
because it makes no sense,
but the Buddha was wrong.
To have even a little love
is better than no love;
there is no greater grief
than to have no love;
that is not only the consummate grief
but the rejection of life;
for not to love, not at all,
is not to live.

It's so natural for us to love,
so unnatural not to.
It took a year or two
before we understood words or spoke.
It took months
before we crawled or walked.
It even took us a while to see,
important as that is.
But what love is,
we knew about that
perhaps before we were born—
and sometimes what unlove is too!

They say that when a man goes without food,
he finally dreams of eating.
But when a man is without love,

I wonder if he has dreams—
or only nightmares?

If a man goes without food,
his body wastes away.
But if a man goes without love,
his spirit wastes away.

Studies made in orphanages have proved
that babies who are not loved
shrivel in mind and body
and fail to grow,
and if they are without love long enough
they die.
Studies made in mental hospitals prove
that adults who do not love
shrivel and fail to grow too,
and if they do not ever learn to love,
they do not ever become human beings.

The principal parts of a verb are supposed to be
the present, past, and past participle;
but if you should ask me the principal parts
of life,
I would say
love, loved, loving,
and the principal part of the principal parts is
loving.
Do you want to love life?
Live loving.

I LOVE TO LOVE

I eat
because by eating I am fed;
I drink
because it quenches my thirst;
I breathe
to keep from suffocating.
But I love
to love—
and all my other reasons for loving
are by comparison
trifles.
I eat and drink and breathe to live,
but I love, to live a life worth living—
and without love I may perish
as surely as without food or water or air,
only more slowly
and more painfully.
For if I do not eat or drink or breathe,
my body suffers briefly
and kills me quickly cell by cell.
But if I do not love,
my soul agonizes long
and kills me lingeringly hope by hope.

Without love
I will not want to live—
and I may do my utmost to make sure
you do not want to live either.

It is just as important for us to love
as for us to be loved.
I am sure we all hope that the one we love
will love us,
but that is not why we love.

We love
not so that we will be loved in return
but because we need to love.

We have all heard the old saw,
"The way to have a friend is to be one,"
and this is probably true;
but it is not the main reason we are friendly.
We are friendly because that is the way we are
made to be;
we are made aching and longing
not only to be befriended
but to be a friend.

I do not love you
in hope to be rewarded by my love.
I love you out of the deepest needs of my
own being.

If I am not loved,
I will not be happy.
But if I do not love,
I will not be human.

Love is a natural force.
We don't have to learn to love,
though we may have to learn how.
We came into the world
wanting to love and to be loved,
needing love as much as food,
and usually getting them together.
To turn off our natural bent to be loving,
we have to be denied, starved, thwarted,
frightened, and crushed—
and even then,
with the least encouragement,
we will start loving again.

HOW WELL DO I LIVE? HOW MUCH DO YOU LOVE?

I will not say you will never weep if you love,
for weep you may.
But this I know—
the tears you shed for love's sake
are not the same as when you shed them for yourself.
They cleanse the eyes of the mists
that come from viewing all things
from the standpoint of self.
Through the tears of love
you see all there is to see
from a different viewpoint
than if you had never loved
and wept for love.
You see what is worth weeping for,
and the unimportance of all unimportant things.

It is strange about the sufferings
you bear for love.
Love makes demands on us,
great demands,
but love is a mystery
and has a power
that there is no accounting for
in ordinary terms.
It is enough that we accept it,
not have to understand it.

The burdens we bear for love,
hard though they be,
are not burdens,
but the means by which we free ourselves
from our own insignificance
and rise beyond our own isolated littleness
to become part

of the universal order
in which alone we find meaning.

Love is compounded out of paradoxes,
and this is one of them:
that out of its suffering
it brings joy
and out of its sacrifice
renewal.

It is when love makes the greatest demands on us
that we find our greatest gifts,
our greatest strength,
our greatest oneness with life.
It is then we gain a sense
that our life has meaning
and serves a purpose.

For the more we give to love,
the more we have to give.
And when we have given all we have
and there is nothing left but love,
what then is left to be taken from me?
If you ask yourself, "How well do I live?"
the answer comes, "How much do you love?"

Not out of love's pleasure,
but love's pain
we may find not loss,
but life's greatest gain.
It is when we have to climb the hard hill road
that we find ourselves closest to heaven.

When we face love's sorrow,
we find love's strength.

LOVE SHRINKS MY EGO

People often mistake popularity
for love—
they are not the same.
No one knows this better
than popular people.
Thousands applaud them
and stare at them as they go by
and stop them for autographs—
and this is pleasant,
but it is not very satisfying
on a lonely night
or on an empty weekend.
It is pleasant to be popular,
to be respected and approved of and honored;
it feeds your ego
and swells your sense of self-importance,
and directs everybody's attention
including your own
toward you.
Love shrinks my ego
and evaporates my sense of self
and directs my attention away from me
toward the object of my love.
Popularity puts me apart from everybody,
out in the center of the arena
or high on the dais
or the platform.
It raises me up above the rest;
they want to carry me on their shoulders.

Love has the opposite effect;
it presses me as close
to the object of my love
as I can get.

I want to kneel before my love
so that my love
may mount on my shoulders,
but when it does,
O miracle!
it draws me up above itself
so that together
we both rise
as one.

Everyone likes popularity,
the way he likes
apple pie
after a full meal.
But everyone hungers for love
the way he hungers
when he is hungry.

VI. Human Beings Always Come One by One

HUMAN BEINGS ALWAYS COME ONE BY ONE

I have known a number of people
who considered themselves very superior spiritually
because, they said,
they had risen above love as something
that happens between individuals;
love for them had become a universal principle,
they said,
which they expressed in a detached, impersonal way
toward all people
instead of a sticky personal way
toward one or two.

But when people tell me they love everyone,
I wonder if they love anyone.
It is so easy to love everyone,
so hard to love any one!
In a very real sense,
everyone is nobody.
For everyone means all,
Eskimos and Laplanders
and Papuans
and Hottentots.
Who has ever seen everyone,
or touched him or heard her
or smelt them,
or even grasped what everyone means?
Stop and think—
What if you had to provide for the needs of
all the people there are!
or comfort them when they hurt,
or bear their anger,
or live with all their small annoying mannerisms?

Imagine what it would be like
to have to give everyone your attention
when you wanted attention,
or let them talk when you wanted to talk,
or satisfy their desires when your own were
not satisfied,
or watch them foolishly doing what they
wanted to do
when you knew wisely what they ought to do
for their own good,
and all the other things
lovers have to do for those they love.

I wonder if everyone
is more than a convenient word
we use when we want to refer
to nobody.

There are almost four billion human beings.
They never have come around in a group—
thank God!—
and knocked at my door
to ask for a handout, or even a hand.
Human beings always come one by one
or two by two
or at most by the dozen.
Even in a vast throng,
at a rally or a ballgame,
I encounter them
one or two at a time.
Only a few can sit behind me or in front of me
or alongside of me
and yell in my ear
or jump up and block my view,
or laugh at my remarks
and agree with my judgment as to what is going on.

Only a few brush against me in the aisle
or come by selling peanuts.

One or two at a time,
hardly ever more,
human beings
please me or irritate me.

One or two at a time,
one or two at a time,
that is the only way human beings
have ever knocked at my door
or entered my life
so that I even had an opportunity
to love them
or not.

So I wonder if loving everyone
is not a gigantic excuse,
and should be redefined as
feeling universally indifferent
toward anyone.

For loving any one—
yes, anyone—
that is a different matter.

For anyone may be the neighbor behind me
who plays his radio too loud on a hot summer night
and the car that cuts in front of me and
steals my parking space
or throws out beer cans onto my lawn
or the rapist
or the Commie
or the pusher selling drugs to my son;
anyone may be any one

of four billion very individual
individuals.

Even those anyones dearest to us—
our father and mother
and husband and wife
and son and daughter
and friend and neighbor—
I wonder how many of us
love any one of them
except part of the time
and a little.

The day may come when I will love everyone—
here and there throughout time
I believe an occasional man
may have grown to that.
But now it is no mean accomplishment
for most of us to love
anyone.

YES TO ONE JOY—YES TO ALL WOE

All my life I have heard how we need
to cultivate the impersonal viewpoint;
if we say yes to one joy,
we say yes to all woe;
if we make room for pity,
we let in all the negative emotions
that will drag us down to ruin.

People point to the imperturbable Buddha
or the impassive Hindu saint,
serene in meditative isolation.
But a clay idol is capable of imperturbability
and impassivity.

I don't think I was made for that.

I think I was made to think excitingly
and feel passionately
and sense keenly
not only my own nature
but my identity
with all that is—
with the world,
with you,
with God—

and when I think and feel and sense that,
that's love.

It is interesting
that the bravest people who have ever lived
have not been those with no attachments,
but those who have had the strongest attachments.
It is the mother thinking first of her child,

the friend thinking first of his friend,
the lover thinking first of his beloved
who makes his stand before the irresistible
and dares to undertake the impossible!
It is the soldier thinking of his comrades
who throws himself onto
the exploding grenade.

It was Leonidas
passionately in love with Sparta,
not the objective Athenian sage,
who stood—and fell
at Thermopylae.

SHE LOVED ENOUGH

Not long ago I read about a woman who was awarded a medal.
She was walking down a city street
when she saw a car careen out of control and come crashing
    down the sidewalk toward her. She saw the plunging car
    in time
to leap safely out of the way.

But thirty feet in front of her
she saw two children
who did not see
the juggernaut roaring down on them.
So she did not jump to safety;
she ran forward
and seized the children
and with all her strength
hurled them out of the way.
She did not have time
to get out of the way herself,
and they gave the medal
to her survivors.

Somehow I do not believe she did this
in a spirit of philosophic detachment.
I think she did it with feeling
running high in her veins,
out of a deep sense of love for life
and for human beings,
perhaps especially for children.
She loved enough
that when the moment came
she was able to give
without taking thought
of herself at all.

A MAN STEPPED OUT OF THE DARK

One night a truck crashed into some trees
off a highway down near Houston.
The driver was caught in the capsized cab
and the truck caught fire.
They tried to get the driver out—
they tied two trucks to both ends of the truck
to try and pull the cab back into shape;
they took crowbars and tried to pry off the doors—
but to no avail,
and the fire began to lick up through the floorboards.

Then a man stepped out of the dark.
He walked up to the truck,
took hold of the door,
and tore it off in his hand.
He reached in and plucked out the steering wheel.
He plucked out the clutch pedal and the brake pedal
and he beat out the flames with his bare hands.

Still they could not get the driver out of the cab.

Then the man wedged himself into the cab
and began to straighten up.
They said you could hear steel popping for miles
as the roof of that cab began to rise
till men could reach in
and pull the driver out.

Then the man disappeared into the night.

They found him a few days later.
He was a negro named Charles Dennis Jones.
A reporter asked him,
"How were you able to do it?"

"You never know what you can do
till you see another man hurting," he said.

I don't think it was imperturbability
that gave Charles Dennis Jones
the impossible strength
to do his impossible deed.
That's unlikely, don't you think?
You see, the year before he had brought home
a string of lights for his Christmas tree,
and the tree had caught fire,
and his little girl had died.
When Charles Dennis Jones saw that driver in that fire,
I think his heart swelled so full
of hatred for that fire
and love for that man hurting
that all the flames of hell
could not have stopped him then—
or if they had,
they would have had to burn him too.

Sometimes I wonder if detachment
ever did much for anybody,
even for the one detached.

But love,
sometimes it blesses
the simplest people.

BUT AS FOR NOW

One of the strangest things about the holy men
who have come preaching love
is that they have usually been celibate themselves
and taught that that was the holy way to live.
But I believe, if we kept account,
we would see that the most likely people
to give up their own good for another
are those who live the usual life
of getting married, making love, and having children.
How often we see lovers give themselves
not only to those they love
but for those they love.
The most selfless acts of sacrifice
have probably occurred where someone gave himself
for his mate
or his children.
Even in the world of animals and birds,
we see creatures mate for life
and live selflessly their whole life long
for each other and their offspring.
Even among creatures where mating is brief,
sometimes we see them
perform acts of great heroism
for their mate
or their offspring.

Every day people give up their own good
for someone they love,
a parent
or a child
or a husband
or a wife,
and sometimes they go on all their life
giving themselves devotedly,

molding and shaping their own life
not according to their own desires
and appetites,
but disciplining and confining their natural bent
so that the one they love may be blessed
and have a fuller life.

It may be that one day we may grow to where
we won't love anyone especially
but everyone equally.
But as for now,
I'll take my chances with those
who have shown they can at least love
one or two—
with a little loving boost on my part
they might add one small person
like me
to their list.

VII.   If I Do Not Have Love

IF I DO NOT HAVE LOVE

If I do not have love,
what do I have?
Do I have hate?
That is an ugly word;
even the most hateful people
shrink from thinking
of themselves as hateful,
and try to justify
their actions.
They tell themselves they are only doing to you
what you would do to them;
their welfare or their safety requires them to
restrain you;
it is merely the punishment you deserve for your acts,
or your intended acts;
they did it
out of necessity,
or even out of love—
for their party,
or their country,
or a lofty ideal.

Some of the cruelest acts men have ever done
they have done in the name of religion,
and put the blame for their acts on God.
They had to torture our body to save our soul,
or they were working to bring his kingdom to earth
and we were the enemy—
what could they do but destroy us?

Even the mad
find reasons for their mad acts.
Sometimes I wonder if the maddest of all
do not find the sanest reasons

to their thinking.
For they have no reason
to require their reasons to be reasonable.
And what is madness
but self-centeredness carried to such excess
that hate and fear
and all the acts they generate
seem reasonable,
and the acts of love
seem mad!

DISEASES OF THE SPIRIT

If I cannot admit that I hate,
will I believe that I fear?
Or will I have to settle for the thought that I am greedy?
Perhaps I would prefer to say
I am indifferent
and have no concern as to what happens to you
or anybody
but myself.
But to be indifferent is not to care
and to be unconcerned is not to feel.

Indifference and unconcern—
these are diseases of the spirit,
and they spread.

When I begin not to feel,
have I not begun
not to live?

I will find it as hard to love myself
when I do not love anyone else
as to keep one cell of my body healthy
when all the other cells are sick.

How many painful centuries will it take
before we learn
that we do not dare to be indifferent
to anyone!
If I am indifferent to the cells in the
soles of my feet
that wearily and patiently carry me about,
only occasionally complaining about their hard lot,
how long will it be

before my whole body
and even my proud superior mind
will be writhing with the pain
that grew from my indifference?

WHO IS KING OF THE WORLD?

A plant and an animal once lived together in a small place that was theirs alone. The plant pressed its long roots down into the moist earth and thrust its long stems up into the warm air. The animal ate the fruit of the plant. This the plant did not mind; it produced its fruit in hope that it would be eaten.

So the two lived together for a long time, sharing their world.

But one day the animal fell to thinking about how superior it was to the plant. "This plant," said the animal to itself, "does not show me the proper respect. It treats me almost as if it were my equal, and as anyone can plainly see, that idea is ridiculous. I the animal am strong and active, and this plant is weak and passive. I can move about freely and it is helplessly fastened to one spot."

So the animal announced to the plant, "Nothing is clearer than that I was made to be the natural ruler of our world. Henceforth whenever I approach, you will acknowledge my supremacy by bowing down and prostrating your stems upon the earth."

Now the plant was not a quarrelsome creature and was willing for the animal to consider itself superior; but to bow down and prostrate itself on the earth would be a hard and unnatural thing for it to do.

"The only thing that makes me bow down is a very strong wind," thought the plant to itself. "While this animal is a blowhard, it is certainly not a strong wind." So the plant continued to send its branches up toward the sun, which was its natural way of growth.

When the animal saw that the plant had no intention of bowing down and acknowledging that it was the ruler of their world, it flew into a terrible rage. It bared its teeth, flexed its claws, and let out a ferocious roar.

The plant paid no heed, but kept right on growing upright.

Then the animal shouted, "I'll show you who has dominion here," and fell upon the plant with tooth and claw. It hacked at the stems and tore at the leaves until nothing remained but a heap of broken branches on the ground.

The animal felt so pleased with its total demonstration of its superior power that it strutted back and forth, pausing only to roar occasionally so that the whole world might know who was the mightiest of all. That night, when it fell asleep, it dreamed happy dreams of dominion and contentment.

The next day when it awoke it was hungry and immediately thought about eating. It took a little while before it realized that its only source of food was now a rubbish heap upon the ground.

The animal ran from side to side in the place the plant and it had shared. But there was no question as to what had happened. It had torn up the plant that had sent forth the branches that had borne the fruit that had been its food.

Then it stopped strutting and it stopped roaring and it sat down dismally on its haunches. "I have made a very grave mistake," it said to itself. It lay down on the remains of the plant and wept that it had been so foolish and so proud.

Its tears trickled down onto the earth and watered the roots of the plant. For the roots of the plant were still there deep in the earth, waiting patiently and acquiescently for their time to grow again.

The animal had hacked down stems and chewed up branches and leaves. But the roots of the plant grew deep down where the animal had no power to reach, and when they felt the animal's watering tears they began to stir in the earth and to thrust up new stems. The stems sent out new branches. The branches put forth new leaves. And in a short time the plant was heavy again with fruit.

But although the plant grew quickly, by the time the fruit appeared, the animal was scarcely skin and bones and its legs were too weak to hold it erect; it lay, an impotent huddle of hunger on the ground, helpless to lift itself up to grasp the fruit.

But the plant, swelling with new life, grew so luxuriantly and gave itself so freely that its fruit bent the branches clear to the ground so that the animal could eat.

When the animal had eaten and felt the life come coursing back through its emaciated frame, it realized how freely the plant gave of its fruit with no thought of holding back because of what the animal had done to it. Then the animal hung its head in shame.

"I had only the power to take life," it said to itself. "I can see now how little that is compared to the power to give life."

UNLOVED, UNWORTHY, INADEQUATE

Not to love—
that is cruelty.
Not to be loved—
that is loneliness.
Not to feel loved—
that is terror.
There is no worse curse
than to feel unloved.
It is a social disease,
not eroding the flesh
but corroding the soul.
We hide the fact we have it,
not only from everyone else,
but even more from ourselves.
I will admit to many shortcomings
and even rascalities,
but to admit that I am not loved—
that I do not dare.
It makes me too vulnerable
to my own terrors;
it turns me into a frightened child
sobbing lonely in the night
for the breast that is not there—
and who can stand to be that?

Before I will say,
"Nobody loves me,"
I will say,
"I don't love nobody!"
I will announce in a loud voice
so that everyone can hear:
"Go away!
I like it here in my corner,
staring at the wall."

I will show you how unimportant
is your love to me.

Not feeling loved
hardly ever comes
looking like
not feeling loved.
She comes wearing disguises.
She is so unacceptable a thought
that we will not let her in
when she comes looking like
herself.

We feel sorry
for the hapless crone
who comes whining how
her mother never loved her
and no one has ever loved her since,
and begs us to let her in
to sit in the dark corner
behind the kitchen stove
where no one need even notice her.
But she will fill the house of your mind
with her mumble of self-pity
till the sound is in your head
like a weary song you don't know the words of
but you can't stop singing.

And she has two sisters,
hags as ugly as herself.
One is called
feeling unworthy,
and the other is called
feeling inadequate.
Once she is lodged in your mind,
she will try to edge them in too.

Those three hags—
are they acquaintances of yours?—
have destroyed more human beings
and ruined more human lives
than all the plagues and pestilences
that have afflicted the earth
since its beginning.

When I was a little boy,
I had a favorite story.
It was "The Ugly Duckling."
I used to get my mother to read it to me
and then I would cry and cry and cry.
My sister felt even more unloved than I.
Her favorite story was
"The Little Match Girl."
Since I have grown up,
I have met so many
ugly ducklings
and little match girls.
I don't think they knew who they were,
but I could hear them weeping
in the winter cold
outside the window.

O all you grown-up children,
who sit rocking yourself
in the arms of your own self-pity,
rehearsing your childhood fairytales
of sorrowful rejection,
it is a sorry thing
to have a sliver
of the Snow Queen's icy mirror
lodged in your heart
so that you cannot love
and never know
why you cannot love—

but the love that will melt
the invisible ice
is your own.

The stone that the builders rejected—
remember that ancient wisdom?—
it became the chief cornerstone.

BEING THE WAY I AM

At the level we have come up to,
most of us are a sometime thing
where love is concerned.
We love a little,
but most of the time
we are engrossed with ourselves
and our own desires.

What is best for somebody else
hardly ever seems like what is best for me,
and in order to do good for others
I have to deprive myself of something,
if only of time and money.
That being the way things seem to be,
you can see why I,
being a prudent and judicious person,
have every right to act the way I act.
Things being the way they are
and we being the way we are,
the way I act
is the only reasonable way
a sane and sensible person
could be expected to act,
don't you agree?

By the time I eat and drink
and take care of my body's needs
and do the work I have to do
to provide myself with a livelihood
and get a little of the fun every man owes to himself;
then add to that
the time I spend worrying about what may befall me
in some future time;
then add to that

the kind of person I am,
tied up in fears and frustrations that make it hard
for me to reach out to anyone else
even when my own needs have been taken care of—
and you can see
I don't have much time left over
for such unimportant matters as taking thought
for the well-being of you strangers
or even of my friends—
if I have any friends,
being the way I am.
But I wonder why
most of the time,
being the way I am, I am
unhappy,
unsatisfied,
and wanting love.

PEOPLE WHO LOVE

I may be able to find people who love
who are not happy.
But I cannot find anyone who is happy
who does not love.

RUN-OF-THE-MILL LOVERS

Being the way we are,
I don't expect people to be too loving,
but I have known two or three people
I thought were very loving.
I have never known any saints,
so I don't know how loving
saints are.
But these people, I would say,
thought about others
instead of themselves
almost a third of the time!
As I say, they were very loving.
They were beautiful people,
they were the most wonderful people
I have ever known.

I have thought about ordinary run-of-the-mill lovers
like myself,
how much time do we spend
thinking about others
instead of about ourselves?
Would you say,
a tenth of the time?
or maybe,
two tenths?

That's not a bad average,
about like a baseball player's at bat,
most of us hitting, say, .200,
with the stars up over .300—
that's not bad in love's league.

And it gives me hope.
The most loving people I personally have known

were—ten?—maybe fifteen?—per cent
more loving than I am.
That made them stars.

O God, I wish I were
one of those stars
in love's league!

I wonder how much practice
loving
it would take for me
to up my average far enough
so that the people who know me
would say when they speak of me,
"He's one of the most loving guys I've ever met!"
I don't think that's what makes people loving,
but I think I'd like that.

SINGING WITH THE SAINTS

I don't believe in a heaven
people go to when they are dead,
but if I did,
I know those thirty per cent lovers I have known
would have fantastic and influential positions
up there now—
it wouldn't even surprise me
if I found them singing
with the saints.

I have thought about that often—
almost in the saint class,
and all they do that I don't
to make that difference
is that they put in ten or fifteen per cent more
love time.

Such a little bit more love,
but oh, how big a difference!

If every man, woman, and child in the world
would do just one more loving thing than he would have done
    in the ordinary course of things, just think,
that would be more than three billion six hundred million acts of
    love!
Wow, what that would do to the world!
It would really sizzle with love for a minute or two;
after a shot of love like that,
it could never quite go back to its old frigidities.

I always sit amazed when I get to thinking of it—
ten per cent more of our time

to being loving,
and our whole world would change.
Even more important,
so would we.

AN OLD LEGEND

There is an old legend
that if you have done any good deed
while you were on earth,
shown any love or charity at all,
you cannot be barred from heaven.
Once there was a rich man—
so the story goes—
who was a mean and cruel miser,
grinding the poor
who fell into his clutches
for their last penny,
and showing no mercy to anyone
no matter how much in need
he might be.
At last he died and arrived at the great gate.
There Peter began to read from the record
one selfish deed after another.
"Keep reading, keep reading," the man pleaded.
"Surely you will find something."
So Peter read on page after page,
until right at the end of the record
he paused.
"Wait," he said, "here is something.
One night many years ago
you bought a newspaper from a ragged urchin.
The paper cost three cents
but you threw the boy a nickel
and when he said that he had no change
rather than wait you told him to keep it."
"I knew it," cried the man.
"I knew I had done something good."
Just then a great voice
came ringing through the sky:
"Is that true?" it demanded.

"Yes, yes, I'm afraid it is, Lord," said Peter.
"Then give him back his two cents," said the voice,
"and tell him to go to hell."

No, the world was made by love
and the principle that rules it
does not want to keep us out of heaven;
it hopes we find our way in.
We have the testimony
of one who ought to know.
He declared:
"Truly, I say to you,
as ye did it to one of the least
of these my brethren,
you did it to me."

COME AND TAKE

Last winter
I put a bird feeder
in my back yard.
Full of love and concern
for all God's little creatures,
I went out in a snowstorm
on a freezing day
and with numb hands
but hands of love
fastened it among the trees.
I filled it with all the seeds
I had been told that birds love best—
sunflower and thistle and millet,
everything a hungry bird might desire.
Then I waited
to see the birds come flocking—
but no birds came.

Oh, the birds were there—
they flew back and forth
pausing in the branches
hunting and pecking hungrily
at any bare patch on the ground below.
But on the feeder
stuffed with tempting viands
no bird alighted.
Once or twice a bird
swooped down beside it for a moment,
gazed at it warily
and with a nervous chirp and flutter
swept away.

I waited till I grew
weary of waiting,

but the hungry birds
went hungry by.

Days passed
before a chickadee flashed in,
seized one sunflower seed,
and flashed away with it.
After that, the chickadee
was a regular visitor.
I liked that tiny black-capped fellow—
there was something about him
that made me think
he was aware of his own worth.
Even when the feeder later
thronged with birds,
he kept up his flashing visits
to seize his one sunflower seed
and fly away with it,
unfrightened even by the bluejays
and indifferent to the general melee.

For slowly
other birds began to come,
first a wary sparrow or two,
then bluejays,
then redbirds, and juncos
and, I suppose, every bird
that heard about it,
for there was usually a crowd of birds
fluttering and chirping in the trees nearby.

But even then,
they came not so much to eat
as to keep one another from eating;
for they spent more time
bullying and scolding,

pushing one another off the perches
than they did
eating the seeds.
They wasted so much energy
being afraid
being angry
and being greedy,
I had a feeling many of them
were going hungry—
though there was more than plenty for all,
and they had only to eat
for me to replenish the supply.

I have wondered
how much we are
like those birds.

I say I believe
love made the world,
but do I live instead
as if I were the inhabitant
of an unfriendly universe
where I have to keep a wary eye
on everything that moves
and most of the things that don't?
And so I scratch and scrap
for every crumb I come on,
almost as anxious to make sure
that nobody else gets anything
as to see that I get my own.

And all the time
there is a principle
that cries out to me,
huddling in my hungry thicket,
"Come and take! Come and take!"

And I have only to come
freely and without fear
and partake of an abundance
ample for my needs
and for the needs
of all who live.

VIII.   Only Love Can Set You Free

I BUILD A WALL

Only love can set me free,
for without love,
I build a wall.

Out of selfishness I build a castle wall
to shut myself in
so that I can have all my good for myself alone.
Out of fear I build a fortress wall
to shut you out
so that you cannot take my good away from me.
Out of hate I build a prison wall—
but then we all dwell in a prison.
That is why we have to wear uniforms.

In prison,
which is the prisoner and which the guard
is often hard to tell
merely by looking at our faces.

SOMETHING IN A BOX

A friend said to me:
"I am like something in a box.
I can peer out of the box.
I can see that there are others like me
in what seem to be similar boxes.
We peer at each other, we communicate.
But I cannot get out of my box.
I can experience nothing
except as from this box.
Tell me how to get out of my box."

I have a feeling there are many
who feel boxed in like that.

We are all prisoners—
first of all, our body's prisoner;
then, imprisoned on the earth
(the moon is merely another cell,
not nearly so comfortable);
and most of all, the prisoner
of our self.

A WAY OUT

Is there a way out?
The saints of the East have taught
the way of withdrawal.
Draw in, they say,
within yourself
till nothing of yourself remains.
When you have dropped away every limiting characteristic
that makes you yourself
and nothing of yourself remains,
then you are not limited by this or that,
but one with all that is,
transcendent, glorious, free.

But I have always wondered about this way.

Better and surer
is the way of love.
The way to rise beyond myself
is not by denying self
but by affirming selflessness.
The Master Jesus taught,
"Love one another."

If I am a prisoner of myself,
who put me in prison?
And who keeps me there?
If I am a prisoner of my self,
what way is there to be free of self,
except to be selfless?
And what way is there to be selfless,
except to love!

Even if you say love does not enable me
to escape from my prison,

at least it enables me to reach my hands
and my heart
out through the bars—
and to touch
you!
You, so like myself—
and holding you, to know
I am not alone.

AS SEPARATE AND ALONE

The trouble with building walls is
that what shuts something out
also shuts something in.
On the inside looking out
we may not be so hungry or cold
as those we shut outside,
but we are just as separate and alone;
even more so, if we shut everyone out—
they have one another,
and we have nobody.
Is there any hunger or cold
so great as separation
and loneliness?
Human beings can stand almost anything but that
and prefer anything to that.
Our worst punishment for hardened criminals
is to put them in solitary confinement,
which is to exclude them from human company,
or to execute them,
which is to exclude them from human life.

Some have thought hell to be fire,
but others have said
hell is an inky blackness
into which we are plunged alone.
In such a state
even a demon coming to torment us
would be welcome.

Has not despair
the quality of emptiness?
To listen but not to hear,
to look but not to see,
to reach but not to touch—

if I had to draw it,
would I not draw empty space
and in it
nothing
but me!

And to turn it into love,
I would need to add
only the lightest brush
of fingertips!

MORE IS ASKED OF YOU

Are you less for having to be more?

Because more is asked of you
than you have so far given;
because you are less now
than you are going to have to be;
because you can see that you fall short,
of your own expectations
and of life's—
would you rather it had been
that nothing was asked of you
and no more was to be attained?
Would it have been a better world
had God made you finished and complete
when he made you
instead of making you so that you have to
complete yourself?
Which child would you rather be,
the child whose mother smothers you with
affection and sheltering,
or the child whose mother sets you free?

Would you rather have love live your life for you
or would you rather have love let you live it
with all its risks, all its failures, all its shortcomings, all its
        stumblings?
If love is love, is there any question
which way it will be?
For love knows that you must find your own way,
though you lose it,
and your own strength, even though you may
be weak;
and it will bid you farewell and send you with
its blessing,

though it knows you go to waste your substance
and eat the husks with the swine—
but with what happy haste it will run out to meet you
when you turn home again
and return to claim your own.

THERE WAS ONCE A MAN OF LOVE

There was once a man of love. He went around the country helping people and teaching them to love one another.

When he met people who were sick, he told them, "You weren't meant to be sick like this. You are the child of love, and love made you. Can you believe that? Then you know that love wouldn't make you to be sick."

When he came on people who were poor, he told them, "You weren't meant to be poor, you were meant to be rich. You are the child of love. Love made the world, and it made a beautiful world with plenty in it for everybody. Can you believe that you are the child of love?"

When he saw people who were unhappy, he told them, "You weren't mean to be unhappy. Love made you. And could love have meant anything for you but happiness? Then believe that you are the child of love and claim your happiness!"

And the people who believed that what he said made sense got a new vision of themselves and their world. The people who were sick were made whole, and the people who were poor found the means to meet their needs, sometimes even in a fish's mouth. And the people who were unhappy began to sing songs in praise of love and of life.

But the people who ran the world did not like what they heard when they heard what this man was saying. If people began to live by love, what need would there be for kings and judges? And even if they still got to run the world, if they had to run it as if it were the kind of world love has made, they didn't know how.

So they got together and decided they had to do something about this smooth love talk and this soft love talker. "He's a public enemy," they told one another. "He'd overthrow all the existing institutions, and that would include us. This man would even abolish death and taxes; he's an atheist anarchist, that's what he is, and we'd be untrue to our responsibilities if we didn't take steps to save the world from his false teaching."

Then they put all their heads close together and they thought, "How can we catch him?"

The people who ran the world were not sure who the man of love was, he was so much like every man. That's the way it is with love, it makes you like those you love. And this man was so filled with love that he was hardly separate from anyone. Since he loved everyone, he had come to look like everyone else and his love brought him so close to those he loved that it was almost as if he were an inseparable part of them.

Then one of the people who ran the world had a bright idea. He said, "We can catch him through his love."

So they found someone he loved and paid him a sum of money to betray him. They said to him, "All you have to do is, when you find him, kiss him. He'll like you to do that because he loves you." Then they all fell to laughing because they thought this was such a clever way to catch the man of love—with a kiss. "That will teach him what love will do for you," they told one another.

So that night the one he loved went up to him and kissed him, and those who ran the world, who had been slinking about in the bushes, came clanking up in their armor and seized him.

Some of his friends wanted to make a fight of it, but the man of love said to them sadly, "Is it for this that I have loved you?" Then they dropped their swords and went away quietly.

When those who ran the world had the man of love, they began shuttling him back and forth among themselves, each one saying to the other, "I think you're the one to take care of this," and each one trying to wash his hands of the matter—for who wants to be responsible for killing love? They expected him to get angry and curse them and create a disturbance, so that they could have a proper court trial. But all he did was look at them with eyes of love, and all he said was, "I love you. I love you all, no matter what you do."

Finally they had him taken out and hanged. They hanged him on a cross instead of a gallows, because that is what they used in those days; it hurt more. But it didn't take him long to die, which those who ran the world thought was just as well.

After he was dead, in a move to pacify any hard feelings, they let his friends cut him down and bury him.

But a few days later, rumors began to creep about the town. It was being said that the man of love they had hanged was still out there hanging. Their spies came and told them this.

"But that's impossible," said those who ran the world. "We had him taken down and buried."

"That may be," said the spies, "but the report we get is that he's still up there hanging high."

"Maybe we'd better go look," said those who ran the world. They weren't sure where to look, but they decided if he was anywhere, he would probably be where his friends were, and sure enough, there they found the man of love, hanging up there high for anyone to see.

"We can see if you want something done right, you have to do it yourself," they said. "And we've certainly got to put an end to this man of love."

For one thing, they knew in their heart that what they had done was a shameful deed and they wanted to hide it from themselves. And for a more practical reason, the last thing they wanted was for the man of love to be left hanging there to become a subject of general concern.

So this time they cut him down and buried him themselves. But in a few days, their spies were back again, saying, "More and more people are saying more and more, he is still up there hanging."

Then the reports that he was up there hanging began to come in from all sorts of places. The rulers of the world were beside themselves. Every time they came on him up there hanging, they cut him down and buried him. "Why doesn't he stay buried like any respectable, law-abiding citizen would?" they asked one another. But he just didn't.

At last they became so angry they decreed that anybody who even reported they had seen him up there hanging, would be hanged themselves. This caused them to hang a lot of people. But in spite of all the hangings, more and more people kept claiming they had seen the man of love up there hanging; and

147

more and more people began to wonder and ask, "Is it possible no one can kill the man of love?"

I wonder myself.

For men are still cutting down the man of love that they hanged, and are still trying to bury him and keep him buried. But he is still up there hanging, no matter how many times they cut him down, no matter how many times they bury him. And from what I can see, he is hanging in more human hearts and more human minds and more human lives all the time. More and more human beings all over the earth are asking, "Is it possible that what the man of love has tried to tell us is true? That the world was made by love, and we are the children of love. And we can live by love and bring forth a world of beauty and health and plenty and happiness, where we can all dwell together free from hate and fear and selfishness, and be the beloved men and women of love."

As I say, I wonder.

For the man of love, after all these centuries, is still up there hanging high, and that's a beautiful and serene smile I see on his face.

I think the time is not far off when the man of love will no longer have to be up there hanging. He will be down here, walking every street, doing every task, meeting every need, transforming every life. As I said, we come to look like what we love; that's why the man of love looks like every man. But the time is not far off when every man will look like him.

IX. They Know Their Own Worth

THEY KNEW THEIR OWN WORTH

As I have said,
I've known one or two loving people.
They didn't talk about it,
they just were.
They put other people first—
part of the time at least.
They did things they thought would make others happy
before they did things for themselves.
They were kind, gentle, considerate.
Before they said or did anything,
they thought about the effect
it would have on others—
or perhaps they did not have to think about it,
they just did what was kind
out of their natural inclination to love.
These people always gave me the feeling
that they understood that no one,
no matter how low on the social scale he might seem,
was less than they;
and so they treated everyone with dignity,
as if he were important.
But I have never known any other people,
no matter how rich or important they might be,
who made me feel they were more aware
of their own worth.
They knew their own worth so well
they did not have to brag about it
or put on airs;
they did not have to belittle anyone
to make themselves big.

Yes, this is an interesting thing about the loving
people I've known—
they always gave me the feeling

they felt no one, absolutely no one
was less than they;
but they also gave me the feeling
they knew no one
was more, either.

THINKING OF URIAH HEEP

I have always questioned people who hold themselves to be
    humble.
When I meet someone who tells me how humble he is,
I cannot help thinking of Uriah Heep.
I've known some people who really were humble,
but I don't think they knew they were.
They just accepted themselves as human beings
like everyone else
and went about their tasks not worrying
whether or not they were different
or superior.

This is the essential quality of humility;
you don't take pride in it.

When people let me know how humble they are,
they only make me aware of how great pride can be;
can there be any prouder pride than this—
to feel that you are superior even to those
who are superior,
not because you feel
you are more than they,
but because you feel you are less!

TO FIT INTO ANOTHER'S HEART

Love may make you small,
but only so that you will not be too large
to fit into another's heart.
Would you be so large
that no one was big enough
to put his arms around you,
or hold you in his thought?
How lonely it would be
to be an elephant
in a world of butterflies.

Sometimes you have to be small
in order to get close
to what you would like to get close to.
I wonder how small you would have to be
in order to get close to a daisy;
no bigger than a bee,
I suppose—
I don't imagine a horse
or a buffalo
would ever get to sip its sweet.

Most of us don't have very big hearts,
and we are careful lest they may be bruised or broken.
You have to be pretty small to get in.
If you are big,
you may be clumsy
when you try to get into a little heart
like mine.
My heart is made of tender stuff,
easy to hurt.

If you push or paw,
I may be frightened,
and may run away.

GIVE YOURSELF AWAY

Love will not give you more.
It may take away even the little that you have.
But love will make you more.
When you love, you do not have more,
you are more.
Yes, though you give away all you have,
and even give yourself away.
For if you love,
you will give yourself away,
holding nothing back.

But when you have given yourself away
so that nothing of your self is left,
then all that is left
is selflessness.

When you are selfless,
you become one with all that is,
identifying not with a little lonely separated frightened thing
but with the infinite.
The spark becomes the fire,
and the wave becomes the sea,
and the leaf becomes the tree.
The leaf can think of itself as a leaf
or as a tree.
Who can say that it is more one
than the other?
But what a difference it makes to the leaf
which it considers itself to be.

There is an infinite difference between
being one

with someone,
and being one
by yourself
alone.

I AM SUCH A LEAF

Suppose a leaf should decide,
"I will withdraw from this tree
into my own true being.
I will isolate myself in silent meditation.
Shielded by my tranquil thoughts
from the perturbations of this tree,
I will go and find myself."

And suppose the leaf did this
and flew off on the wind
till it came to rest
on the forest floor?
Will it not find that it cannot find fulfillment
as a thing complete in itself?
As a thing complete in itself,
separate from the tree,
it is nothing but crumbling dust
in a dusty world.

Only as it gives itself to the tree,
reaches out to sunlight and rain,
lets the life of the tree pass through it
as it grows and unfolds,
only then does it have meaning
and find fulfillment.
What happens to any other part of the tree
affects it,
and what happens to it
affects all the tree.

On the tree of life,
I am such a leaf,
and I fulfill myself

by giving myself to life
and letting it flow through me
to make me and life
more alive.

FROM ITS LIMITLESS MUCH

Love will not leave you less
than what you are.
Love takes what you have to give it,
hungrily, insatiably.

But although love takes,
love also gives;
and however much it takes,
love gives more;
for love takes from your limited little
and gives from its limitless much.

Love is like the flame
that takes from the candle
tallow
and gives to the candle
light.

X.   Something in Us Tells Us

BLIND CORNERS

A bird flies into a room.
We open all the windows
and try to edge it toward one.
But often it continues
to flutter blindly
from corner to corner.

The windows are open.
Nothing restrains it
but itself.
The whole sky beckons
if it will but fly forth.

So we flutter
about the little room
in which we find ourselves,
come to blind corners
in our reasoning,
beat vainly
against the windowpanes
that are our senses.
Yet the windows are open
on infinity itself
if we will but fly forth.

ONLY TO MAKE ROOM

We go on living our little, hard, self-centered existence,
while the whole universe cries out to us:
Love and you will be loved.
Give and it will be given to you.
You are not made less but more by all that you give
and when you have given all that you have to give
and nothing remains,
what then can be taken from you?
What bondage can be put on you who are already
the bondsman of love?
Give without holding back
and there will be no limitation
except the limitation you put upon yourself.
In the ancient Greek story
of Baucis and Philemon,
the pitcher that served the gods
never ran dry,
no matter how much was poured from it.
And in the ancient Hebrew story
it was only when the widow ran out of jars
and had no more to set before Elisha
that the oil ceased to flow.

Love may ask you to give up many things
you would prefer to keep.
But if it does, it is only to make room,
perhaps not for greater things,
but for greater growth.

Things are blessings when they enable us
to enjoy what there is to be enjoyed
and to accomplish what has to be done.
Then they give us freedom and power.
But sometimes they encumber

rather than enable us;
they clog time and crowd space
and make us prisoners in our own world.
Love can set us free
from the tyranny of things.

SOMETHING IN US TELLS US

How long will it take me to learn?
We all have to give ourselves,
every accumulated bit of knowledge,
every possession,
every title,
every achievement,
every atom.
Sooner or later we have to return it
to whatever we drew it from.
We can hold nothing back.
To the extent that we learn to love,
we give willingly
and we go willingly;
we become a harmonious part of the harmonious process,
taking and using and returning and giving.
Otherwise we hang on,
screaming or crying or cursing or whining or raging,
to no avail—
it will be wrenched from our reluctant grasp.

The world has made us so that there is no way
we can hang on to self.

Where is the self we would hang on to?
Would you be the babe, the child, the youth, the mature man
        or woman, the bent oldster?
And do you think there were fewer changes
before you got here,
or there will be fewer
after you leave?
You were never more fixed than you are now,
and you never will be.
Metamorphosis
is for more than frogs and butterflies.

Even if you could,
how long would you wish to be yourself?
Can you consider a more dreadful doom
than to have to be you
as you are now
for eternity?
or even a million years?
or even a thousand?

Before we have the power to live a life
unlimited in duration,
let us pray that we have the power to live a life
unlimited in capacity
to change and grow.
Before we go to live with the birds,
we must first find wings
and learn to fly.

As long as I hang on to self,
I will be asked to give it up.
But when at last I let go,
I find I had nothing to let go of.

We hang on to self so desperately
because we are afraid of selflessness.
We scream at having to be born.
When we are a boy,
we are afraid of becoming a man.
When we become a man,
we are afraid of old age.
And once we become old,
we are afraid of what lies on the other side of that.
I cannot let go of old truths
even when they no longer meet my needs.
I cannot let go of my little self
even when it brings me mainly pain.
My familiar nothing

is better than the unknown everything.
Perfect love may cast out fear,
but fear shuts out even imperfect love.
It draws inside itself
and pulls its hole in after it.

Like the seventeen-year locust
fear hugs its dark root underground
when all the time
it was meant to be a flying thing
and rise on wings.
How does it gain the courage at last
to crawl up into the air?
And we, how do we learn
to go beyond selfish ends
and to give ourself to something more than ourself?
For here and there one of us learns,
and lives his life for more than himself.
His aim becomes, not his own gratification,
but the greater good of others—
one other,
a few others,
a community,
a nation,
humanity,
life.

Then we mutter about what a good person we have known
or even talk about a hero
or a saint,
and wonder why we don't have the courage to do it, too;
for something in us tells us
it is the way we are meant to live
and it is the only way we will ever become
what we were made to be.

SELFLESS SELF

When we love,
we go beyond our little self
to selflessness,
which is perhaps the best name
for our true identity.
Then we become alive
in a way we cannot know
when we are isolated fragments of life.
As long as we are self,
we must have all the limitations of self,
we must be born to self and die to self,
we must find our self and lose our self,
we must grow and change and become.
But when we become selfless,
we are immortal
in a sense we cannot understand or grasp in terms of selfhood.
We become one with the transcendent being
out of which all individual existence emerges,
and one with the immanent being
in which all existence is included.
When we pass beyond self,
we attain to selflessness.
That is not to be less but more,
as a stream is more when it loses itself in the river
that embodies many streams
and the river is more when it loses itself in the sea
that is the consummation of all the rivers.

For when the littleness in us grows less,
the greatness increases.
When we are no longer bound
to selfish ends,
we are free.

When the separateness in us is dissolved,
we are at one.
When we let go our limitations,
we find ourselves beyond them.

And beyond them is God.

As beyond a wave there is the sea
and as the wave is not separate from the sea
but extends back into the sea
and shares the sea's strength,
so beyond body, beyond mind,
there is the selfless self
where each man knows
that he is not separate and little and powerless
but one with the Omnipotent Good itself.

XI. Moments of Love

OF ALL THOSE VANISHED MOMENTS

How important is love?
Consider for a moment
all the moments of your life.
Which ones do you remember?
Of all those vanished moments,
what few had significance enough
that now, as you reach back for them,
they return?

Everyone, I am sure,
can remember a few moments
when he did something he wanted to do,
won a victory,
made a discovery,
had an adventure.

If you were the president, for instance,
I am sure you would remember
a few crowds cheering you, some election nights,
perhaps some crises in government
or confrontations with important people.

If you were a general,
you would surely remember
a few moments in battle.

For myself,
looking back and trying to recall
events important enough
to have stuck in my memory,
it is amazing how few there are.

I remember the day I ran away from home,
got on a bus and went to college,

in a red suit with $63
safety-pinned in a vest pocket,
all my worldly belongings.
I can still roll down
U.S. #40 Highway on that bus
and read the road signs,
if I close my eyes.

I remember the night
I was elected student president.
When I found out I had won,
I went into the men's room
and got sick.

I would have thought
when I started counting memories,
I would have had a lot connected with my writing—
it has always been the most important thing in my life—
but I don't.
I can remember a few funny stories
about how I came to write this or that piece—
that is all.

I remember how I came to get the house I live in—
maybe because it was a kind of miracle.

Oh yes, and I can remember when I was ten—
that was the low year of my life!—
I ran out into the street and a car came slamming down the hill
        and hit me.
I have always thought we had an appointment—
he needed to hurt somebody
and I needed to be hurt.
I can still remember
flying up into the air spread-eagled over that black coupe
and coming down on my head on the curbstone.

And as I ransack my brain,
more and more such incidents
begin slowly to seep up.
I am sure if I thought hard,
I could bring back a score or more.

But it is amazing,
as I sit and let the memories sift back,
how few are connected with what I would have told you
were the important things that happened in my life,
the big events—
times when I achieved something I wanted very much to achieve
or got news of some advancement
or made a lot of money.

No, the memories that come flooding back
aren't important memories at all.
They are just memories connected
with people I have loved.

BIG JIM AND LITTLE JIM

I remember—
you know, I don't believe I have a memory more meaningful
    than this—
rising as a small boy
early in the morning, while it was still dark,
and going down into the kitchen of my grandmother's house
with my grandfather—
oh, the golden hours we spent together,
big Jim and little Jim!
I would help him start a fire in the coal stove
and he would cook breakfast for us both,
a heaping plate of fried potatoes and eggs!
it is still my favorite breakfast.

I remember when I was supposed to be dying with the flu
after the First World War,
and I had a screaming nightmare—
the devil had come for me
and when he turned around in his red suit he was Santa Claus!—
and my mother came in
and got in bed with me
and held me in her arms.

I remember being with a friend and being chased by a gang of
    older boys
and running up a hill
and coming to a big rock
too big for either of us to climb—
and I boosted my friend up over it,
and he promptly ran away and left me.

I remember when I was a teen-ager—
oh, that's the time when you have the friends!

friends you are certain will be friends forever—
and where have they gone?
I can remember getting up early in the morning
with a couple of boys I loved
and hiking across the fields and through the woods,
just to watch the sun come up and be with one another.
And I can remember going up with them
to the Liberty Memorial late at night,
and sitting on the high stone wall there,
where we could look out across the city,
and talking until sunrise.
It is interesting,
I don't remember any of the great things we talked about,
though I know we must have been witty and profound—
I just remember talking with my friends.

I remember the first time I kissed the girl who became my first
     wife.
I remember the first time she saw the sea—
she had never seen the sea—
we came striding across the dunes at Barnegat,
and there it was,
and she caught her breath
and sat down under the sand dune
and she never said a word—
hours must have passed!—
and still she sat and sat,
saying nothing, only staring
at the pounding breakers and the endless expanse.
I remember, I remember—
some memories that I would remember,
and some that I would forget.
I remember how I sat and sat
outside her room in the hospital,
saying nothing, only waiting,
listening to the sirens screaming,
carrying pain to paincastle.

I remember standing beside her bed in the morning
and watching her breathing
grow less and less
and stop.

I remember the first time I ever made love to a woman.
There wasn't much love in it,
but I remember.

I remember being a godfather a couple of times
and a best man a couple of times
and a number of funerals.

I remember the first time I kissed the woman I am married to
    now.
We were going up in an elevator
and I wanted to kiss her and I thought she wanted to kiss me
and we did
and the elevator
went up and up and up
and so did we.

I remember riding with her on a summer night
in an open car
when the stars shone like flowers in her hair
and cicadas and crickets sang serenades around us
and the new-mown fields were a perfume,
and I reached and touched her hand
and we held hands and we rode
through a summer night not made for sleep
but for dreams and lovers,
and I still ride down those roads
under those stars
hearing those songs
in that summer night—
a thousand rousing dawns have not washed it from my brain.

I remember the first time
I ever rocked my grandson in my arms
until he fell asleep.
And I remember the first time
I pointed out the moon to him,
and a few days later,
as we were walking in the garden,
suddenly he pointed up and said,
"Moon, Grandpa,"
and sure enough, there it was,
a pale day-moon of a moon!
And he reached up his arms as high as he could reach,
and he said,
"Give it to me, Grandpa!"
and I wish I could.

MOMENTS OF LOVE

These are just a few of the memories I remember.
As I just said,
when I started out to think of memories,
I thought they would be the big important events
that would come hustling into my brain,
but they weren't,
they weren't these at all.
They were just a few passing moments
shared with someone I loved.

And an interesting thing about the great moments of love,
they may not be happy moments.
Some of the moments I remember best
were probably the most anguished of my life—
but they are the moments that give life most of its meaning.
Joyful or painful—
I don't believe that's what's important.
What's important is
they were moments of love.

Moments of love,
only moments—
sometimes one or two such moments
are all that remain
of a long lifetime.

A few moments of love,
these give life most of its meaning.
Without such moments,
life would be almost nothing,
no more than the smoke that has vanished
of a fire that has gone out.
We manage to love one or two people,
and this little love makes the difference

between bare existence
and a purposeful life.

What then would life be like
if we could love a hundred—
or a thousand—
or ten thousand—
or the whole human race!

A few moments—
when you embraced your wife,
walked in the woods with friends,
sat with your dog at your feet,
watched a dear one die,
held your grandson in your arms—
a few moments,
hardly more than this!
But above the darkening unremembered plains
where we have crossed,
they shine as we look back,
and they warm our heart
and cast a soft glow
over the long dark strange journey
that we make not knowing why we make it.
They are the times—
these little times of love—
when we came alive and lived.

O God,
what if we could hold the whole world in our arms,
and care for its needs,
and tend its pain,
and share in its joys—
yes, and in its sorrows,
even in its sparrow-falls!
How deeply, how intensely,
how meaningfully
we would live then!

I'M LOVING THEM

We get to thinking so many unimportant things are important,
and not the things that really are.
One day a mother brought her baby
out onto the front porch
where his older brother was playing,
and told the boy,
"Watch your baby brother for a few minutes."
The boy sat down beside the basket
and after a while his puppy came running up
and lay down at his feet.
As they all sat there, a neighbor came by.
He looked at the boy and the baby and the dog
and he said to the boy:
"What do you think you're doing there, young man?"
The boy looked at the man and said:
"I'm loving them. I'm loving them."

SHE LETS US LOVE HER

Just to be loving.
Just to be loved.
How few of us know
that is enough!

My dog is very much a dog;
she does nothing
except what a dog should do,
which is largely nothing.
She is not even an especially affectionate dog—
she does not leap on us
when we come home
or cover us with wet kisses;
but in a quiet way,
like some human beings,
she shows us that she loves us.

She is a beautiful dog,
though not even that in everyone's eyes.
But she does none of the things
we human beings have come to feel
are necessary:
she does not possess a fortune;
she does no useful work;
she has no fame
or important position in the community;
she shows no exceptional talent.
She does no great feats
so that we can brag about her to the neighbors.
She does not even guard the house
or do clever tricks for company.

She does only one thing—
she lets us love her.

No more than this,
but this is enough.

She needs no other reason for being
except
to let us love her.
Love justifies all the expense and care
we lavish on her
and compensates us for the nuisance
she sometimes is,
like every living thing.

Just to be loved.
Just to be loving.
This is reason enough for being.
Have you ever thought of that?

You there pursuing so intently
all those grand schemes
and lofty ambitions
you feel you have to pursue
in order to be of value—
you there striving so hard—
for what?
My dog lets me love her—
no more than this—
and that is reason enough—
and more—
for her to be.

How glad I am
that we found her
and have her living with us.
My wife and I are willing to be
her maid and cook and nurse and companion and provider.

There she lies
stretched out indolently on the floor
and she lets me pet her,
if I will take the trouble to bend down.

I look at her
and I know something
more about life
than I knew without her.
I know what is necessary and important—
and what is not.

XII.   Because I Love You

IDENTIFICATION

What is love?
Before I finish this book
I ought to say what I think it is.

There are two elements in love.
The first of these I call identification.
That is a big word by which I mean
I tend to become one with what I love.
They say that two people who are happily married for a long
    time
come to look like one another.
I have also heard that people tend to look like their dogs.
That might be a natural consequence of identification, I suppose,
but not an inevitable one.
Identification is not just look-alikes;
diamonds look a lot like glass, but they aren't the same.
We become one with what we love.
Spit on my country's flag and you have spit on me.
Kick my dog and my body quivers with humiliation and rage.
Insult my friend and I'm the one you have to fight.

If I love you,
what happens to you happens to me.
I laugh when I hear your laughter,
and I weep to feel you hurt.
The trumpets of your triumphs blow for me
and your defeats are wounds I also bear.

To love is to share,
but to love is more than to share.
To love is more than living in the same house
or even living together.
It is growing together in a mystical way

no one exactly understands
or can describe
though we all know how to do it,
without having to be taught.

OTHER-MINDEDNESS

The second element in love
I call other-mindedness.
By this I mean,
that I think of you instead of me
and put your well-being above my own.
Instead of being anxious about myself,
I am concerned for you.
I devise ways of serving you
instead of contriving ways of self-serving.

So it is that my petty pains
and minor troubles
are seen in their right perspective.
The more universal our love becomes
the more clearly we see ourselves
in right relation
to everything else.
It is said that God feels when a sparrow falls—
would you want him to feel less?
His mind is with us all,
and so is his heart.

SYMBIOSIS AND SYNERGY

Scientists like to talk about symbiosis
and synergy.
Symbiosis is
where two creatures get together
each doing his own thing
but between them making a way of life for both
better than either could make it alone;
and synergy is where
two substances combine
like nickel and steel
and form an alloy
stronger than either of them alone,
or both of them considered separately.
That's the way it is
when we love one another—
symbiosis plus synergy plus the mystery of love.
When I love you,
I don't just add to your strengths
and subtract from your weaknesses;
I don't just attract your friends
and repel your enemies.
My loving you
changes the conditions of existence for us both
so that the whole business of life
is conducted in a new and happier frame.

IN HOPE OF A SUMMIT

I do not love you in hope
that by loving you I will get you
to do what I want you to do.
I do not love God
in hope that by loving him I will get him
to do what I want him to do.
The opposite is more likely to be true.
Because I love you, I will do
what you want me to do.
Because I love God, I will do
what he wants me to do.
Because I love,
I may have to do things
I would rather not do,
and I may not have to do things
I would rather do.
Love makes demands
and places restraints.
I love
because it is my nature to love.
I love
because though I have all the world
and have not love,
I am as one hungry and naked in a wilderness
lost and seeking,
crying for love
even when I do not know it is love
I am crying for—
getting but never satisfied,
giving but finding no peace in the gift,
running from thing to thing
and from gratification to gratification,
climbing a hill that has no top,

going down a road that is always disappearing
around another bend.

But when I love,
it does not matter what road I may go down,
or hill I have to climb,
for I do not go down the road in pursuit of ends,
or climb the hill in hope of a summit,
but for the one I love.
To love the one I love—
that's all the end I want to reach
and all the summit I hope to climb to.

NO RIDER OR RIDDEN

When I love you,
though I be the beast that is ridden,
where would you go
that I would not wish to take you,
and where would I take you
that you would not wish to go?
When I love you,
there is no rider or ridden,
there is no driver or driven,
there is only the beloved bearing the beloved
and there is only love guiding love.

IF I HAD A LOVING HEART

If I had a loving heart,
you would not go hungry when I had food,
you would not go lonely when I was near,
you would have no pain when I could lessen it.

BECAUSE I LOVE YOU

When I love you,
I find my happiness making you happy.
I say the things you like to hear
and do the things you like having done for you.
And I say and do these things not to make you love me,
but because I love you—
and so I love to say and do them.

LOVE NEVER INSISTS

I may hear what you say before you say it
because I am listening—
not only to hear what you say
but to hear what you do not say
but only yearn for in the silent secret chamber of desire;
for lovers touch without having to reach,
and reach without having to touch.
I feel what you want before you tell me what you want,
because I want it for you.
I do not force my wishes on you;
what I want is for your wishes to become my will.
I make no demands on you,
not even that you let me show my love.
How can love place the one it loves in bondage
even to love?
If I love you,
I do not insist
on your being anything
but what you are.
Love never insists,
love entices.

I OPEN THE DOOR OF MY HEART
BUT I DO NOT MAKE YOU COME IN

If you do not come up to my expectations,
I do not lessen my expectations
but neither do I lessen my love.
I appreciate you,
so I help you to appreciate yourself.
I know your worth,
so I help you to know your worth;
you see it shining clear
when you look into my eyes.
Because to love is to stand close,
I am always near at hand
if you need help;
but I don't intrude.
I open the door of my heart
but I do not make you come in.

LOVE ONLY HAS TO BE THERE

One of the hardest things for love to do
is to keep from pressing itself
on the one it loves,
for love is drawn to the object of its love
as the moth is drawn to light—
but who of us wants moth wings
fluttering about his face?
Love should be close, but not hover;
be mindful, but not too solicitous;
be attentive, but not overwhelm with attentions.
Sometimes the best thing for love to do
is nothing at all—
love only has to be there
loving.

THERE WILL BE DISTANCES

But let no one tell you
there is a need
for distances in love;
the distances will be there
without your having
to make provision for them.

Love is closeness.
When I love you,
there will be distances
and separate things will happen to you
and to me,
but they will not happen
to one of us alone.

LOVE IS THE HEART'S VIEW OF THINGS

When I love you,
I accept you as you are,
because you are what I love.
If you grow to be more
because I love you,
I will rejoice in what you come to be.
But I shall see you perfect
in spite of flaws;
for love is a way of looking
not at outer forms and appearances
but from heart to heart.
Love is the heart's view of things,
and so it sees us
not as we seem to be
but as our heart intends us—
and ask your heart,
is that not always good?

Do we have affinities?
I cannot say,
but this I know—
every single atom longs for love.
It roams the universe
seeking out the particle
with which its whole being craves to be united
and when it finds it
hurls itself at it
with an irresistible force
and clings to it
with a passionate tenacity
as if this were its true state
and it were not a separate thing,
but composed with its companion part
a single object.

LINKED IN RHYTHMIC BALANCE

No man knows why
atom seeks out atom.
We talk about electromagnetic attraction
and the law of gravity
as if that explained anything.
When the universe demands,
"What name shall I write down?"
polysyllabled words and complicated equations
are just the way the learned scientist has
of marking down his "X."

We talk about positive attracting negative
as if we knew what we are talking about.
Could positive be the masculine
and negative the feminine
aspects of reality?
though it may just as likely be the other way around—
it's getting harder to tell boys from girls all the time.
All we know is that particle seeks particle
everywhere
till they are linked in rhythmic balance,
circling round each other
in beautiful harmony—
could they be dancing
in each other's arms?—
singing (so the scientists tell us)
if we had but ears to hear them—
love songs?

XIII. Love Is a Passionate Pursuit

SOMEONE TO HOLD

The ideal state, I suppose,
would be for the whole human race
to love the whole human race.
But we haven't come up to that just yet.
Not long ago when I took my wife in my arms,
she looked up at me and said,
"I wish everyone in the world
had someone to hold."
What a happy thought!
If we all had someone
or even something
that was dear to us
to hold,
what a difference it would make to us—
and to everyone,
yes, even to those we don't love.
When I hold my wife
or my grandson in my arms,
I wouldn't let go of them
even to take advantage of my worst enemy.

FROM NONE TO ONE

To love even one,
how far we have to come to come to that!
From none to one
is an infinite distance,
so the mathematicians tell us;
but from anyone to anyone
is farther than it seems,
and we need no mathematics books to measure
the loneliness of onliness.

LOVE STRIPS US NAKED

To expect people to be loving all of the time
is to expect more than anyone I've ever known
is capable of.
To expect people to be loving some of the time
is to expect a lot.
We human beings cannot stand to love
more than a little
and occasionally.

We are afraid of love.
Aren't you afraid of love?
Oh, a little love is all right—
enough for family and friends
when you need them—
but a lot of love,
that's another matter.

Love strips us naked,
doesn't it?
We have to love
and be loved
for what we are then—
not what we seem to be
when we are all dressed up
and in our office
or our drawing room
or in our limousine
driving home from the bank.

There aren't many people
we are going to trust
to see us naked,
not even our bodies,

let alone our souls—
love strips them naked, too.

Sexual love
is the symbol
of what all love has to be.
It strips us down
to our fundamentals;
we have to enter a relationship
as one with one
at the basic base of our being
and find fulfillment
there.
It is not an accident
that "to know"
originally meant
to have sexual intercourse with;
for love demands
that we know one another,
not know about one another
as we might learn from a book
or a conversation,
but by the most me I dare to be
encountering the most you you ever let me know
and pressing as close
to one another
as the two of us know how,
searching for oneness.

When we are making love,
there is not much we can hide behind
or pretend about.
You have to want me
at just about the most basic level
of my being
and I have to want you the same way,
not for anything you bring

or anything you give
or anything you own,
not for honor
or riches
or convenience
or advantage,
but for each other
only.

MANY WAYS TO SPELL IT

Maybe that's why it's so hard to love
even one or two.
Love doesn't ask a little.
Love demands a lot.
There are many synonyms for love.
Love is a little four-letter word,
but there are many ways to spell it.
I'll stick to l-o-v-e, though I might almost
say g-i-v-e.
Some people use the dirty words.
Some people use the Greek words.
Some people use words like
like and affection and fondness and friendliness
and good will and fellow feeling—
and these are all good words,
but not good enough.
They suggest a handshake
and a pat on the back
and somebody saying of somebody else,
"He's a fine fellow, don't you think?"
That's what is wrong with the Greek words
the theological fellows like,
agape and *filia* and *eros*—
they are like the brass labels on museum cases,
and sound as if they have been dead for 2000 years.
That's what's wrong with most of the words for love—
they have no passion in them.

I THE HUMAN BEING
COME WITH MY HUMAN HEART

Love is not passion,
but love that has no passion in it
is not love.
It is no more love
than an artificial rose made in Hong Kong
is a live and fragrant bloom.

Love is a fire,
and fire, I have observed,
does not inquire politely of the fagots,
"Do you wish to burn?"
Love may not stand
and knock at the door
on a windless summer night
and beg you to come down
and let her in.

Love, and you may find yourself
rising from your bed at night
to wander down strange ways
that you did not even know were there
and where you had no wish to go,
asking all whom you meet,
"Have you seen him whom I love?"
And when you find him,
you will not be able to let him go
but will follow him
wherever he may take you,
not because he bids you come,
but out of love's necessities
at the bidding of your own heart.

Love is not a sentimental journey,
love is a passionate pursuit.

When I love,
I the housewife
come warm to my husband's desires.
I the husband
come gentle to my wife's needs.
I the mother and father
come with reassurance when my children question and demand.
I the nurse
come with patience to my patients.
I the teacher
come on fire to teach even when my students have no wish to
     learn.
I the worker
come running to my rendezvous with work.
I the human being
come with my human heart
to comfort the human sorrow
and bind up the human pain.
I the man of God
come with no thought of self to do Compassion's will.

Love is not an intellectual thing,
or a matter of fulfilling the requirements—
the soldier snapping to attention
or the worker punching the time clock.
Love entwines the lover and the loved one,
the soldier and his duty,
and the worker and his work,
in such a tangled net of consciousness
that no one can be sure
whether one answers because he hears the other
call in need,
or whether one calls because he hears the other's
need to answer.

XIV.   A Man and a Woman

WHAT IS DEAREST TO US

That is why, in spite of all the theological treatises and ca-
    nonical injunctions,
I appreciate the sentiments of the two Irishwomen who were
    leaving the cathedral,
and one turned to the other and said,
"Wasn't that a glorious sermon
the Archbishop just delivered
on the joys of married love?"
"Yes," said the other,
"and I wish I knew as little about the subject
as he does."

In spite of all the celibate sutras to the contrary,
the love of a man for a woman
and of a woman for a man
is still the best and highest and most unselfish love
most of us are capable of—
and at its best,
is there anything on earth
that is more beautiful?

The great love stories,
are there any we like better than these?
Sometimes happy,
sometimes tragic ones—
that doesn't seem to make much difference.
Why do we hold them dear
except that they speak of what is dearest to us.
The great lovers—
fact and fiction—
we love them all!
Because we know
they have had something
that gives life meaning and makes it real,
however it turns out in the end.

AFFIRMATIVE AND CREATIVE

The love of a man for a woman
and of a woman for a man—
this is the most universal expression love finds on earth—
affirmative and creative in its aspects,
probably the principal source of human joy,
certainly the only source of human life,
an expression that most individuals need,
if they would be happy and unfold their powers,
and the whole species needs,
if it would preserve itself and evolve—

I do not believe
that this expression
is not as holy and beautiful a part of life
as a narrow life
of denial
and prayer.

WISE AND UNWISE ACTS

I realize that many acts performed in the name of sexual love
have nothing to do with love,
and sometimes not much to do with sex—
but this is true of everything we human beings do.
To breathe fresh air,
to drink cold water when we are thirsty,
to eat when we are hungry—
what is better than these!
But we can eat and drink and breathe
to poison our body and mind
and destroy our life
and the lives of those who love us.
Love of country,
how good that is!
and how many hideous crimes have been committed in its name!
And in the name of love for God,
what dark deeds have been done—
the tortured souls of ten thousand faiths
cry out against the wrong.

Out of love of God
and love of a human being,
out of religious love
and sexual love,
we can do wise and unwise acts.

AN EXCESS

We do not love at all unless
we love passionately—
but passion and love are not necessarily the same.
An excess of religious passion becomes fanaticism.
An excess of patriotic passion becomes chauvinism.
An excess of sexual passion becomes lust.

Uncontrolled appetite soon controls us
and unbridled passion mounts us and whips us where we would
    not go.
Thus, the love of God has often led to fasting
and from fasting to silences
and from silences to flagellations
and from flagellations—
to flagellating all the world!
Likewise, sexual appetite
has led its miserable devotees
from one sexual experience to another
until there is no curious excess
excessive enough to satisfy.

TO HIDE OUR SEX IN SHAME

It is hard for me to believe
that God disapproves of sex
when he has made flowers,
which are the sexual organs of plants,
the loveliest and daintiest and most fragrant of living forms!
I wonder what sin we human beings have committed
to have to hide our sex in shame.

It is interesting that the language of sexual love
and the language of religious ecstasy
are so much like one another
that the church Fathers put a lovesong
celebrating sexual union
into the Bible as a holy book—
and is it not one!

And the holiest of saints
have addressed God as their bride
or their bridegroom
and described in erotic phrases
the ecstasy they felt in his embrace.

A PRAISE OF SEX AND LOVE

Surely God meant sexual love
to be a psalm of joy-in-life,
a song to celebrate
our body's power to give and take delight.
It is a song no one has to teach us to sing—
the music is written in our cells.

Full of grace notes and pleasant surprises,
it may be sung in several different keys;
but it is most beautiful
when the dominant note is trust
and the song begins and ends on the tonic chord
of mutual respect and understanding.

It is not a choral number,
God wrote it as a two-part song.
When two sing happily together
and practice till they grow familiar with the tune
and one another's change of pace and variance of style,
then hidden overtones and harmonies emerge,
at once intense and delicate,
small heightenings of sound too subtle to be written down,
but the Composer hoped the singers
would discover and draw them forth.

Then the song becomes what he meant it to be,
rising tuneful note by note
through dolce and crescendo
to a glorious hallelujah,
thence subsiding at the end
into a great amen of peace.

XV. The Most Important Things

THE MOST IMPORTANT THINGS

When the king died, he found himself being taken to wherever it is kings are taken when they die. I don't mean his body. He had left that along with his robes and his crown and his throne and all his other possessions back in the royal palace.

As he found himself floating along, he naturally wondered what was going to happen to him now.

The Cardinal had always been a little evasive when the king had tried to question him about the matter. His Eminence had politely implied that kings got a special dispensation. But the king thought he said it more as a matter of politics than anything else—he said it with so many hems and haws.

The king had heard all his life that he was supposed to go up above the sky to a beautiful city, that is, if he was eligible to get in—and the king had never doubted this—or believed it either. But as he thought about it now, he didn't feel that it was outward through space that he was floating, it was more as if he were floating in great depths within himself.

But however that might be, he would soon find out where he was being taken, and he felt reasonably sure about his prospects. He had been a good king, at least he thought he had.

He had gotten to be king in the time-honored way, his father had been king and before that his grandfather, so there was no question as to his credentials.

His courtiers had addressed him as king of kings and whenever there was a parade his people had shouted after him as he went by, "Long live the king!" as if they meant it.

He had done the usual things expected of a king, he thought. In fact, he had been rather kingly. In his youth he had fought a couple of wars, and they had turned out as successfully as most wars do; the country had gained a little property, and lost some men and money. In the battles, he had taken his chances with the rest of them, and he felt he had conducted himself rather admirably. He had even won a couple of medals; he liked to wear them when he dressed up for special occasions.

However, he had not been a warhawk. He was glad of this. He had an idea it might be to his credit wherever he was going.

After the second war, he had relied on negotiations and alliances to get his country what he felt it needed. He had married his three daughters off to neighboring kings, and felt that he was good friends with all of them.

His own country, he had left in the hands of his only son. The thought occurred to him that his son was king now. His son would miss him, he thought, but not so much that it would interfere with his joy in getting to be king. He remembered how he had felt when his father had died, and he had gotten to be king!

And his son already had a son. So it looked as if he had left the country well taken care of for a long time.

Only the thought of the queen made him feel sorry about what had happened. She really would miss him, he believed. After all, he had been her husband for forty—let's see, yes, forty-seven years! And a darn good husband. Yes, he had been.

Then, too, she wouldn't be queen any more. She'd liked being queen. However, she'd make a good queen mother. All the children liked her—better than they had him, he thought. But his grandson liked him better—at least, that's what he felt. And she felt so, too. She'd told him so.

Wherever he was going, one thing was sure—he'd miss her. No doubt of that. He had depended on her.

But he hadn't had time to miss anything yet. He was too busy going wherever it was he was going. Suddenly he realized that he hadn't had time at all. The moment he had left his body everything had ceased to happen, so somehow it was still the last day of his life. But time had lost its meaning. Floating along in the involuting emptiness he seemed to be in, there was nothing to measure time by and whether a long time or no time at all had been passing, he could not say.

So he was not sure just when it was that he became aware that he was not alone. He did not see anybody; he looked around. He just felt—a—a presence.

It was slightly eerie. He saw nobody. Nothing. But he knew

something was there. He supposed this was the sort of thing he would have to get used to.

Then he heard a voice—or was it a voice? It was hard to be sure. It might have been a thought rising out of himself. He had always been one to talk to himself a lot.

The voice said: "Hello, there!"

The king said: "Hello! But where are you?"

"Oh, I'm right here!" said the voice. "I am always forgetting. You don't see me, do you?"

"Who—who are you?" said the king.

"I'm your guide," said the voice. "You'll get used to me shortly. Just relax. You've come through a tremendous change, and it's natural to be a little upset. I'm here to see that you find your way."

"My way where?" asked the king.

"That's what we have to find out," said the voice. "It's too early to be sure. But as we go along, everything will be straightened out."

"You think things are going to be all right?" said the king.

"Perfectly right. You can be sure of that," said the voice.

"I—I was king," said the king.

"Yes, I know," said the voice.

"I was wondering, isn't there a special place for kings?"

"Did you like being king?"

"Yes, yes, I'd say I did. Everybody told me I was a good one."

"They usually do," said the voice. "And you can be sure, we try to put everybody where he belongs."

The king was not sure just what that indicated. "Is there a court that decides what's going to happen to me?" he said. "Am I judged?"

"We don't like that word," said the voice. "We'd prefer, guided."

"And you, you are the guide?" said the king, peering intently in the direction from which the voice seemed to come, although it hardly had direction, for it seemed most of all to come out of himself. "I was expecting an angel."

"What makes you think I'm not one?" said the voice.

"I don't see any wings," said the king.

"You don't see anything," said the voice. "But we'd better get along with the guidance, hadn't we? It's not going to be anything hard. What determines everything is the three most important events of the last year of your life. What would you say they were?"

"I—I'd have to think," said the king. "But don't you want to consider my whole life? I really think the most important things I've done I did a long time ago."

"The last year is all that concerns us now," said the voice a little sharply. "What you did fifty or sixty years ago may not tell us at all what you're likely to do now. And we're trying to find out where you're going now, isn't that right?"

"I suppose so," said the king.

"Very well. Let's begin. What would you say was the most important event of your last year?"

"Oh, that had to be my Golden Anniversary as king. I was king fifty years, you know. Not many kings do that. Important people from all over came to the ceremonies."

"This was important to you then?"

"Sure," said the king. "Wouldn't it be to you?"

"If I were king for fifty years, I wonder what would be important," said the voice. "But it's easy to find out. It's all recorded on the importance scale. Let's find it. Golden Anniversary as king—ah, here it is. It registers almost 4. The scale runs from 1 to 10, by the way."

"Importance scale—what's that?" said the king.

"I didn't tell you about that. Everything that ever happens to you leaves an impress—every thought you ever think, every word you speak, every word spoken to you, everything you do, everything done to you—every happening—it all registers on you —deeply if it's important, lightly if it's not. And all these impressions determine what you are and how you react to anything. That's the theory the whole eternal process runs on. So, all we have to do is find the three most important things that happened to you recently, and we have a pretty fair idea of what you're like, and where you should be going."

"I just told you," said the king. "This Golden Anniversary— that was number one."

"No. I'm afraid it wasn't," said the voice. "Not according to the scale. Here is something that made a much more important impression than that. Let's see. You were having a big meeting. At your suggestion—a good idea, by the way—the rulers of twelve nations had come to your city to form a league. You gave a formal address of welcome at the opening meeting."

"Yes," said the king. "That was important. I agree with you there. I believe I'd put it up close to the top of the list."

"The meeting? Good heavens, no," said the voice. "It hardly registers two on the scale. But when you came back to the palace, your cat was dying."

"Boots?" said the king.

"Boots. Yes, that's his name. You had brought his basket into your room."

"I had to do that," said the king. "He'd been getting sicker and sicker. And he was such a proud, free fellow. He'd always come and gone as he wanted and had the run of the whole grounds. Now he couldn't. So I brought him in to stay with me."

"How long had you had him?"

"Twelve years," said the king. "He came as a little kitty. I never had liked cats. They're cruel, you know. But I was out walking in the garden one Sunday and I heard a meow. Down out of one of the big trees came this little kitty. A handsome little fellow, all black except for his face and his four white boots. That's why I called him Boots. He was catching and eating grasshoppers, completely self-assured, not asking any handout. He came up to me and thrust out his paw in the most dignified way you ever saw. I could almost have sworn I heard him say, 'How do you do?' Oh, there was never any of that 'your majesty' stuff between us. When I was with him, I was never sure which one of us was king.

"I had ordered that any cats found on the grounds be taken

229

away. But this little fellow had this tremendous something. He took himself for granted, and I could see, assumed I would. And I did, didn't I? I kept him. Twelve years."

"You loved him?"

"Yes, yes, I did. I respected him, too. I think he loved me—in his own way, at his own times. Yes, deeply I think, deeply. He was my friend. It was the sort of friendship two men sometimes have. Not depending on each other, but admiring each other and complementing each other. A kind of quiet bond built on something that goes very deep."

"You came home after this important meeting," said the voice, "and you found him almost dead."

"Almost. I could tell. I never knew what had sickened him. I took him to all the doctors. But they didn't know either. I always thought maybe something had bitten him.

"When I came home that afternoon, I sat down by his basket on the floor and began to pet him. I'm not sure he even knew I was there. He was slowly growing cold. But I petted him and petted him, I don't know how long. I petted him till I knew he was dead.

"The queen came in and found me there, sitting by my cat.

"'He's dead,' I said.

"She put her hand on my head. 'I've got to bury him myself,' I said.

"I found my old jacket in the closet, that I had worn when I was a young man and gone off to the wars. It still had some of my ribbons on it.

"I wrapped him in that as tenderly as I knew how. Then I took him downstairs into the rose garden. The queen came with me.

"It had begun to rain, but I found a spade in the tool shed and I dug a hole among the roses. That was hard work. I was soaking wet with sweat. I had to stop two or three times. I'm not as young as I once was. Hey, that's a joke now, isn't it?"

"Yes," said the voice. "I believe you are younger right now than you've been in quite a few years—sixty-four, isn't it? Then you buried him."

"I buried him. I broke off three roses and buried them with him. I filled in the grave, and then I turned to my wife, and I began to cry. I guess I cried pretty hard. I am a funny crier. I don't cry easy. But when I start, it comes out of me in great racking sobs. And curses, too. I usually curse when I cry. She held me in her arms until I stopped. And she kept saying, 'That's all right, that's all right, that's all right. You just cry.' And she patted me as if I were a baby. I guess I was, wasn't I?

"Then we went upstairs holding onto one another, and I changed my clothes. They were a mess. And washed my face. I had to hurry back to those meetings. I had another speech to make."

"That was a very important happening," said the voice. "It registers almost at the top of your importance scale."

"But that's not the sort of thing you look for from a king," said the king. "A king ought to have something more important on his mind than a cat."

"I am not looking for anything, I am just looking for what's there," said the voice. "Let's see. Here is another. Yes, this impression goes deep, too, very deep. This happened right at the end of your Golden Anniversary."

"I told you, that was an important event," said the king.

"When all the fetes and parties were over," the voice went on. "You and the queen were tired, very, very tired."

"It got pretty boring toward the end," said the king.

"You decided to slip away," said the voice. "So the two of you went alone to a little villa you had down by the sea. You went to bed early, but sometime after midnight—it must have been three or four—you woke. The room was full of light. You got up quietly so that you wouldn't disturb your wife, and went to the window. A full moon was dropping down the western sky, its light streaming across the sea. That was a beautiful moment to you. Underneath the roaring sea where the waves were foaming on the rocks, and over you this glorious yellow moon, slowly drifting down through little jagged clouds, sending its long silver ribbon of light dancing on the water toward you. You even rhymed, 'The moon like a snail has left a silver trail.'"

"Not a very good rhyme," said the king.

"No. But apt. Then you felt a hand touch yours, and you knew that your wife had gotten up too and come to stand beside you. You turned and saw her there in the moonlight, her long hair loose and streaming down, and you drew her to you and kissed her. And the two of you slipped down upon the floor and there by the sea under the moonlight you made love to her."

"Why, you're nothing but a damn Peeping Tom," said the king.

"Please," said the voice. "Nobody was watching you. We are not spies here. I am reading only what you have recorded in yourself."

"I don't like it," said the king.

"Was it or was it not important?" said the voice.

"That was a night!" said the king in a tone that left no doubt about it. He floated silent for a while. His mind was not on where he was going, but in a villa by the sea.

"Those two are at the top of your list, or just about," said the voice at last. "But we need one more. Yes, here it is."

"Something big?" said the king hopefully.

"Very. Very. Yes, on the very last day, the day you—uh—uh—"

"Of course," said the king, "that is an important moment, isn't it?"

"Oh, I don't mean your dying," said the voice. "That happens to everyone—and almost everyone takes it in stride—for what it is—an inevitable and not too surprising incident. It changes conditions, it doesn't change you."

"But that's the only thing that happened that day," said the king. "I felt sick at lunch, I went upstairs, I had that sharp pain, and then—"

"No," said the voice. "Not that at all. That hardly records as a tremor here on your importance scale. But something did happen. Something that left a tremendous impression on you.

232

That last day. It seems to have been a very high day in your life. It started early and rose in the impress it left on you until almost the end. Yes, till that lunch."

"But I did nothing," said the king. "I spent the whole day playing with my grandson. His mother brought him over in the morning. He had told her he wanted to be with Grandpa. As I told you, I think he favored me."

"And you, didn't you favor him?"

The king gave a quiet chuckle. "It's interesting. I had had the same kind of relation with my grandfather. I'd rather be with him doing nothing than with anyone else doing almost anything. And I think that's the way it is with my grandson and me. I suppose he'll be very sad."

"For a little while," said the voice. "Don't you remember how it was when your grandfather went?"

"Of course," said the king, a little sadly. "He's so young, in a short time, he'll hardly remember me, let alone the silly little times we had together."

"Probably not," said the voice. "But that doesn't mean you haven't made a deep impression on him. Look at the impression he leaves on you. You will forget the events, too, just as he will. I assure you, you will. But you'll always carry the impression engraved on the very fiber of you. I have a notion he will, too. What did you two do to have so rare a time?"

"Nothing, like I told you," said the king. " 'Let's go for a hike in the woods, Grandpa,' he said. So that's what we did. Just the two of us. We strolled along cutting off dandelion heads with a stick and listening to the birds and watching them fly about. Every time a bird flew by, he'd say, 'What kind of a bird is that, Grandpa?' And I'd tell him, even when I didn't know. You see, he thinks I know everything. I hope my telling him I knew what those birds were when I didn't isn't held against me."

"Not by me, it isn't," said the voice.

"Thank you," said the king. "He picked dandelions and any other flowers he saw. He'd come running with his hands full of them crying, 'Look, Grandpa, look.' And I would have to

233

take them and thank him and tell him how beautiful they were. I guess all children do that, don't they?"

"I hope so," said the voice.

"There is a clearing in the wood and in the clearing a small pond where lilies grow around the edge," said the king. "He loves that pond. I suppose it's ocean-big to him. Goldfish live in it, and he always runs around the bank, pointing them out to me. This morning he got a long stick and pretended he was fishing. I happened to notice that the edge of the pond was laced with tadpoles. Thousands of the little black squirming blobs were swimming around and over one another. When I pointed them out to him, he tried to catch them in his hands. Together we dug a little hollow there on the bank and filled it with water and he dumped his captives into this. I don't know how long we spent, but at last he had collected quite a number.

" 'You're quite a fisherman,' I said.

" 'How many are there, Grandpa?' he asked proudly.

"I counted them, one by one; there were ten. 'Ten,' I told him.

" 'Is that a lot?'

" 'Oh, a great lot. You can see that!'

"He beamed with pride.

" 'They're tadpoles,' I told him. 'When they grow up, they'll be frogs.'

" 'When I grow up, will I be a king like you, Grandpa?'

" 'Yes,' I said. 'Yes, you will. Do you think you'll like that?'

" 'Will I get to ride your white horse, Saber?'

" 'You'll have all the horses you'll want,' I said. 'And anything else you want.'

" 'Anything?' he said. 'Will you come and play with me then?'

" 'Oh, you'll probably want something a lot better than that,' I said.

" 'When I am king, what will you be, Grandpa?'

" 'You don't have to worry about that,' I said. 'Grandpa will always take care of himself.'

"Some steppingstones ran out into the pond, and I had never let him walk on them before. But he begged me to let him, and

I thought, 'He has to some day.' So I let him. That was something to watch. The way he hesitantly put a foot forward, then drew it back, thrust it shakily out again, and then suddenly screwing up his courage, took the step! As he gained each stone, he would turn around and look at me to see if I was appreciating the magnitude of his feat.

"'Bravo! Bravo!' I cried. 'But you be careful there. If you fall in, your mother will spank both of us.'

"Suddenly, of course, in he went. I had him out in a second. But we were both soaked. A wind had come up, and it was chilly.

"'We have to be getting back,' I said. 'Maybe we can sneak in and change your clothes and your mother won't see us.'

"His eyes shone at the thought of outwitting his mother. But we had hardly started back before he stopped and said, 'I'm tired, Grandpa. Carry me.'

"So I carried him piggyback up to the palace. It was too far, I suppose. But he was having a wonderful time, and he kept kicking me with his heels, and wrapping his arms around my neck till I choked, and shouting, 'Giddyap, Grandpa! Giddyap!'

"And I tried. I neighed and snorted and ambled along like the old horse I am—or was?"

"Was," said the voice.

"He'd scream and shout, 'Faster, faster!' And so we came romping and laughing back to the palace. I was breathing pretty hard. I suppose I shouldn't have done that, should I?"

"On the contrary," said the voice, "you certainly should have. From the impression it left on you, I don't believe you've done anything more important. At least, not for a long time."

"Well, that's about all that happened," said the king. "I got him up to my room and after I got some fresh clothes on him and got dressed myself, he crawled up on my lap, and he said, 'Bounce me on your knee, Grandpa.'

"He is getting to be such a big boy, he wears his old Grandpa out. But he whooped and hollered as long as I went on, so I went on as long as I could.

"At last I said, 'Hey, there, your old horse needs a rest.' So we just sat there and I held him on my lap for a long time. Suddenly he turned and threw his arms around me and said, 'I love you, Grandpa.'

"And I said, 'I love you, Prince Snicklepuss.' He liked me to call him that.

"His mother and my wife came in about then and we all went down to lunch. I knew at lunch I wasn't well, and after lunch I came back up to my bedroom again—and you know what happened then."

"That rounds it up," said the voice, "the three most important events of your last year. The death of your cat, making love to your wife on a moonlit night, and a walk in the woods with your grandson."

"It doesn't sound very important," said the king. "You're sure that's it?"

"We never make a mistake in such matters," said the voice. "There is nothing else that happened to you last year that even came remotely close."

"Wasn't there even one epoch-making thing I did that you could count?"

"You saw me unroll the record. You saw what counted."

"Does it mean then that where I'm going I won't be king?"

"I don't know about that," said the voice.

They floated along silently awhile.

Suddenly the voice said, "We're just about there!"

"Where? Where?" said the king excitedly.

"Where you're going."

"It—it's good?" said the king.

"Very good," said the voice. "It's where you can be you."

"King?" asked the king.

"If that's what you are!" said the voice. "One thing you can be sure of, it's the place for a man who loved his cat, his wife, and his grandson. Ah, we're there!"

The king felt a surge of life roll through him, a rush, an overpowering wave that drove him precipitately on his way.

236

"Good-by," said the voice. "It's been nice knowing you." It sounded a long way off.

The king tried to say good-by, but he couldn't. Suddenly he had a breathless sense that he was pouring headlong and pell-mell down a vast and confusing funnel, and at that instant he passed through the point at the center and—and—he couldn't remember a single thing that he was trying to remember, not even who he was, but it did not seem to matter. All that mattered was that he had emerged and was alive—beautifully, vitally, fully alive.

In fact, he had just been born, and he let out a startled cry.

XVI.   The Love of Power and the Power of Love

IF I HAD A WISH

If I had a single wish,
I would wish for a loving heart.
At least I hope I would.
I would be afraid,
shiveringly afraid—
I would hesitate for a long time,
but I hope in the end I would have the courage
to make that wish—
for a loving heart!—
if I had a wish.

To wish for a loving heart—
that is a very great
and very hard
wish to make.

Is there anybody
who is not afraid of love?
When he loves,
he is going to be asked to give—
and that is tricky, sticky,
and fraught with peril—
who knows what you will be asked to give?
Doesn't everyone hang back?

I have always thought
that the most courageous statement in the Bible
is where Isaiah hears
the Lord say,
"Whom shall I send, and who will go for us?"
And Isaiah says,
"Here am I! Send me."
It has taken me a whole lifetime
to say that

in a faint whisper
hoping no one will hear,
most of all God.

Why am I so afraid of him
who is love?
It is the strangest
contradiction!
What could love wish for me
except my highest good?
What could love do to me
except bless me?

But I guess there is nothing
we human beings do more reluctantly
than give.
We would like to give,
we want to think of ourselves as generous,
but when the time comes
for us to stretch out our hand
with the gift in it,
we remember an important engagement we had
in another part of town
and most of us most of the time aren't there.

There is nothing more human—
and there is no point in feeling guilty about it,
that just adds feeling unworthy to feeling unloving—
but there is nothing that keeps us
from living life to the full,
having the life we might have,
more than this holding back from giving;
for to give is not only to love,
to give is to live.

Do you know what love is going to ask me to do?
Love is going to ask me

to love.
Yes, to love.
And that is what I want to do more than anything else in the
world,
and that is what I am afraid to do more than anything else in
the world.
Love is going to ask me to love
and to give.
For to love is to give.
Love does not have to ask—
when I love
I cannot hold back from giving.
If I love enough
and if my love desires,
I will give all I have,
even myself,
even my life.

I would be afraid,
oh, very much afraid,
if suddenly I knew
I was going to have
a loving heart.
But if I had a wish,
a single wish,
that is what I would wish for.

THE GREATEST BOON

It seems impossible
anyone could think
that a loving heart
is the greatest boon
anyone could have,
if anyone could have
anything he wished for.

There are so many things everyone wants—
riches of course and health
and a long life to enjoy them.
Then there is fame—
most of us would like that:
to perform some great achievement
that the world would applaud—
make a great scientific discovery
that would win, say, a Nobel Prize
and benefit the human race
or write a poem or a symphony
that would touch deep chords in the heart.
If I were a girl,
I might want to be so beautiful
that no one could see me without desiring me—
though being a man,
the wish to be the handsomest and strongest
seems a long way down the line as wishes go.
As a man, however,
I might want to be king of the world.
King of the world—
that sounds as if it would be gratifying.
The wish for a loving heart seems pretty humble
alongside a wish like that.
But pleasant as all these other things are,
you could live without any of them.

But without love—
at least a little love—
I am not sure you could live at all.
And I am sure,
it would not be a life worth living.

OH, I WISH FOR A LOVING HEART

If I were king of the world,
that would be pretty wonderful.
I could have almost anything I wanted—
money and jewels and beautiful clothes
and castles and automobiles and airplanes and yachts,
and people bowing and scraping and waiting on me
and flattering me—
crowds would wait in the rain just to see me drive down the
     street.

I could make people do anything I wanted them to do,
or if they wouldn't,
I could keep them from doing what they wanted to do
and make them sorry they hadn't!
I could give beautiful things—riches and honors—
to anyone I liked,
and take them away from anyone I didn't like.
I have to admit, all those things
are things much to be desired.

What would I get from a loving heart
compared to kingly joys like these?
I'm afraid, I would *get* nothing;
a loving heart is not concerned with getting;
what it knows is how to give.

And yet
I wish,
oh, I wish
for a loving heart!
And if I were king of the world,
I wonder
if I wouldn't wish for a loving heart
even more.

SIEGFRIED AND CHRIST

Most of us decide,
somewhere along the trail,
that power is better than love.
They are the two great human figures, aren't they?
The man with the sword
and the man on the cross,
the upraised fist
and the outstretched hand,
Siegfried and Christ,
the man of power
and the man of love.

Love and power—
they are both desirable.
The Hindus believe
that when a man develops his spiritual powers
through lifetimes of unfoldment
to such a pitch that he has the power
to become a savior,
he will be born into the world with a choice—
he can become the savior
or a world-king.

When the Buddha was born,
his father knew that his son
had been born to be a savior,
but he knew also that this meant he might
become world-king.
There was no question
in the father's mind
as to which
is to be preferred.
So he surrounded his son
with all the things he thought

might whet his desire to be king—
pleasure palaces
and dancing girls
and race horses
and beautiful gardens.
He taught him to hunt
and ride and fight.
He saw to it that he should experience
all the ten thousand joys of this world
in the hope that they might woo him
to seek the power
to obtain yet more of them.
He carefully kept from his sight
any of the ten thousand sorrows of this world
that might lead him to wonder
whether the joys of this world
and the power to have them
are the pure unalloyed fun
his father was trying to convince him they were.
But the gods were not to be deprived
of their savior—
possible saviors do not come along all that often!
They saw to it that the Buddha saw
three sights:
an old man,
a sick man,
and a dead man.
This is your inevitable destiny, they said.
The joys of the world will bring you to this,
yes, even if you are king of the world.
After that,
the prospect of kingship
lost a little of its savor;
and when he caught sight of a monk
begging on the corner
and looked into his eyes
and beheld in their depths

untroubled peace
and serene detachment,
he knew that the powers of a king,
however many dancing girls
they might briefly provide,
were not so much to be desired
as the peace of a beggar.

THE PRESENT PROSPECT

A million years
of having to look out for ourselves
or perish—
a million years
of having to scrounge for food
and going hungry,
of having to watch out for hostile bears
and human beings,
of being beset by floods and droughts
and pestilence—
this million years
of self-preserving selfishness
is lodged in the back of our brain
holding us back from giving ourselves away
to anything.

But the present prospect
of plenty for everyone
and nobody having to go without;
with most of the bears locked up in the zoo,
and most of the floods dammable
and most of the droughts floodable
and vaccination for almost every pestilence except the common
    cold;
the present prospect
of rockets and atom bombs
and nerve gas and biological warfare
that may go off anywhere an ill wind, bad aim,
or a misfire carries them;
and everybody on earth
living only a few minutes
from everybody else;
of everybody being better off
if everybody prospers

because that's the only way to keep the
machine running,
and the knowledge that pestilence
is no respecter of national boundaries
or even of stone walls around the estate
if the family down the street is living
over a garbage dump;
the present prospect
of imminent anguish
if we keep on living
as we have for the last million years—

this present prospect
plus that million years of self-preserving selfishness
is beginning to gnaw at the front of our brain
making us wonder if maybe
we are going to have to look out for others—
or perish.

IT GETS WEARY SLEEPING ON YOUR SWORD

Most of us abide by the laws most of the time—
and we expect everybody else to be law-abiding, too.
However, we know they are not,
so we have police.
We are willing to treat people justly
in order to have them treat us justly, too.
We have learned that life is better in a world
where laws govern us
than in a world where force rules.

In a world where force is the only law,
even the strongest and bravest and cleverest
does not often survive to a peaceful old age;
there is always an ambitious youngster who would
like to measure himself against him,
and see if he can't become King of the Hill himself.

The game called King of the Hill
is one of the oldest
and bloodiest
of human games—
and it is fun to be king for a while
but it gets weary
sleeping on your sword half awake,
leaping up at the lightest footfall
or even an imagined one.
And even if you prove too fast and tricky for an ambitious
    youngster to pull down,
the rest of us band together some dark night,
willing to risk the lives of two or three of us,
in order to maintain the life of all.

Human beings learned to do that a long time ago.
That was the only way they could master

dinosaurs and saber-toothed tigers
and violent human beings.

No, we learned a long time ago
that life was a lot easier
and a lot more pleasant
if we would live it by some rules of conduct—
even rules that worked out in such a way
that the most aggressive of us—
the strongest and bravest and cleverest,
the king and the nobles—
would get most of the goodies.

For most of us
a life governed by laws,
even poor laws,
was still much better
than a life governed by force,
which really meant a life of perpetual fear.

So we set up laws.
But love—we haven't come that far yet.

CAESAR GAVE IT A SHOVE

Up until now, men have almost always chosen power
as a way of solving problems,
individual or international.

We have tempered power with law,
but in the final question,
we rely on power.

Rome tried to found a world on law,
but there was no love in Roman law,
and so there was no hope of order and peace
for these can come only out of love.

The world that was founded on the law
that was founded on might
overturned
when Caesar gave it a shove
and the grandeur that was Rome
fell from Octavianus, Augustus Imperator,
to Nero, fiddler,
to Caligula, monster,
to Heliogabalus, weakling,
until at last the impotent Emperor of Rome
bought his auctioned-off throne
from the palace cutthroats
who then killed him
so that they could sell it
to another.

Rome was built on power
tempered by law
rather than law
tempered by love,

as I hope is the case with us,
however much we still rely on power.

They were trying to be just, I believe;
we are trying to be merciful, I hope.
Perhaps neither they nor we have often achieved either
justice or mercy,
but they tried,
and we are trying.

For I believe with all my faith
that man is meant to live
not by power but by love.
Human beings are going to keep falling over themselves
until we meet the challenge we have to meet
not by destroying those who challenge us
but by loving them.

For power is powerful
and might is mighty,
but the power by which we destroy others
also destroys us,
and the might we use
to press down others
in the end presses us down.

There is a universal law—
to every action
there is an equal and opposite reaction.
How can we hope to evade it?
Do we think the law will be suspended
especially for us?

As far back as we know anything about—
is that three or four thousand years?—
we have seen nation after nation
win the war—

that would end war,
that would destroy the enemy that had to be
destroyed,
that would make them safe and secure
for a thousand years—
only to see the nations they defeated
rise up renewed from their own ashes
to bring them down in revenge;
or to see their mighty strength
become so overwhelmingly overweening
that it had nothing left to do except to turn on itself
in civil strife;
or to see their strength,
drained by the effort
demanded for the victory,
slowly and helplessly
dissolve and disappear.

Egypt, Assyria, Macedonia, Rome,
the Arabs, the Tartars, the Mongols,
the Ottomans, Spain, France, England—
shall I add the United States of America?—
how many more must humankind see come and go
before they have learned
that hate can produce only hatefulness
and force can only raise a counterforce
and beset by itself
trickle down
and dwindle
till it is
nothing.

IT IS INTERESTING

"God is on the side of the biggest battalions,"
said Napoleon,
but it is interesting that this little man of power,
after many victories
in which his big battalions
became smaller and smaller,
ended his little life
on a tiny rock in the Atlantic,
miserable, ill, and alone,
not even having power enough
to be master of his own mind
or his own body.

Rome, the haughty, cruel, and beautiful empress of the ancient
        world,
who sat on her seven hills
and stamped the earth into submission
with her marching legions,
was raped by a rabble of barbarians,
most of them Romans,
and today is no more
than a few ruins
for tourists to gape at.
It trusted in its power—
and its shattering excess of power
broke it to pieces.

But the man Rome crucified,
whose only power was love,
is still changing lives
and influencing people.

IT FENCES ME IN OR OUT

Power exerts its force on me
from the outside.
It takes the shape
of the king's scepter
or the bully's club.
It shouts threats and commands,
pushing me back
and telling me
where I cannot go
or what I have to do.
It fences me in
or out,
and makes me snap to attention
or fall down on my knees
when it goes by.
It works by giving favors
or taking them away,
frightening me with its concentration camp
and firing squad
and the midnight knock on my door
by the secret police.

But since power always comes from the outside,
I can keep it there.
It cannot get inside me
and find out what is going on there.
So I can fight power
with guile,
and even occasionally
drop a tile from a rooftop
or mail a letterbomb.
When the power becomes topheavy,
it is easy to undermine.

And I have allies
I am not aware of;
the way the world is made is on my side.
For power
that has no love in it
sooner or later becomes
merely the power to inflict pain.
When this occurs,
the whole world
marshals its resources
to protect itself.

OUT OF LOVE

Force works from the outside in.
It uses blows and threats,
so I recoil from force;
I may give in to it,
but I do not give out much.
What I do because I am forced to,
is never more than I have to do;
slave labor always turns out
to be the least productive.

Love works from the inside out.
It uses my own desires;
it does not make me give,
it makes me want to give.
Force has to make me give anything;
love has to make me stop giving everything.
What I do because I love to,
is always all I can do;
love's labor always turns out
to be the most creative.

There are limits to what you can force me to do.
But who has set the limits to what I will do for love?
To care for those they love,
men spend their life
at tasks they hate.

Out of love
men give their life to God,
or their country,
or a cause,
or a vocation,
or a person.

Out of love of God,
men have spent their life on top of a pillar
or in a cell
or kept a vow of silence
or let themselves be tortured and burned.

Out of love of their country
men have gone to their death
not being dragged by force
but running and singing.

Out of love of a cause,
men have given up all they had
and borne imprisonment
and public scorn.

Out of love of a vocation,
men have worked endless hours all their life
for almost no gain.

Out of love of a person,
men have given up vocation and cause and country and God.
They have abandoned hope of fortune in this life
and hope of heaven in the next.

When love asks love,
"What do you want to do?"
love replies to love,
"Whatever is in your heart to do for yourself."

BUT UNLOVE—WHO CAN ACCEPT?

I have known men hungry for power.
They were all men who despaired of love,
and I believe that it is only when you lose the hope of love
that you gain the need of power.
In the same way, men hungry for money
seek it not for the money
but for the power it gives,
and they need power
because they could not find love.
With money you can buy favor,
and with power you can command attention,
but these are not love.
I imagine that those who depend on money or power
tell themselves
that those who run to do their bidding
run
out of love.

What lonely longing must pour out
from what lonely men
on what lofty thrones
in what eagle posts of august isolation—
in the solitary confinement of their souls
behind the locked doors of their hearts
guarded against intruders
like love,
even if there were love—
through the barred windows of their brain
peering for any sign of favor,
even feigned,
even bought!

To be unloved—
this is a state not one of us can bear.

To be poor,
to be ignorant,
even to be ugly—
this we can endure, however painfully.
But unlove—
who can accept?

If all I have is power,
do not be surprised
when I, the almighty and alone,
out of my great unlove
begin hurling thunderbolts.

If you do not love me,
I will try to see
that you will love nobody else,
for I will make a world,
if I can,
where nobody loves
nobody—
where every man turns against every man
in strife and fear and war and pain.

THE FLYWHEEL WOULD FLY TO PIECES

It is not power itself that is wrong.
The question is not one of love or power,
but of whether I use the power
for the sake of power
or the sake of love.

Power used for its own sake
breeds more power,
until it is overpowered
by its own massive excess of power.
But power used for love
breeds more love.

If there were no wise external restraint
supplied by the governor,
a flywheel would gather so much speed
and generate so much power
that each particle of the wheel
would fly so fast
and become so powerful,
it would rise up and insist
on being recognized as pre-eminent
over every other particle—
and the flywheel
would fly to pieces.

So far no person
and no people
have used power
for its own sake
and survived their power.

Rome was not overpowered by barbarians
until it had been overpowered by Romans.

How shall I spread the pestilence
and stay immune to its deadly touch?
How shall I drop the atom bomb
and escape its contaminating horror?

I wonder,
is it impossible to turn your power against others
without having it turn against you?
Is it impossible to live for yourself
without yourself dying?

WHERE HOPE LEAPS UP

Machiavelli,
like the Buddha's father,
advised the prince
to choose power over love.
For you cannot make anybody love you, he taught,
but you can make everybody fear you.
As to love, he was right;
but in the second case,
he was wrong,
as many a prince
trusting in terror,
has found out too late.
Machiavelli should have said:
You can make everybody feign fear of you.

If your power depends
on your power to hurt me,
you had better learn to sleep lightly;
you have taught me to hurt you
if I have the power.
And you cannot rule by fear
without being ruled by it.

Has there ever been a tyrant
who did not surround himself
with bodyguards and food-tasters?
When you only dare let me look at you
through bullet-proof glass,
I have a feeling that though the glass may not shiver,
you do.

When your power depends on love,
that does not guarantee
that you will have no enemies—

266

Machiavelli is right,
you cannot make everyone love you.
But if your power depends on love,
it means that you are loving—
what more does it need to recommend it?

I cannot describe how great is the difference
between ruling and being ruled by love
and by fear.
A life ruled by love
and a life ruled by fear—
they are as different as the lives
of two different species.

Have you ever felt fear?
I do not have to ask that, do I?
Most of us feel it much of the time,
not quite screaming panic,
not quite quiet desperation,
just the slight unease,
the almost imperceptible tremor,
the sudden creaking sound at the back door of the mind,
that sets the flesh on edge, wondering,
could something
be there
trying
to get
in?

Have you ever felt love?
I do not think I have to ask about that
any more than about fear.
Most of us feel love once in a while,
not quite heaven, perhaps,
but not earth either,
the warm bubbling up of our highest spirits
and a joyous feeling of entering unrestrainedly into life;

the quiet sense that all is well
however things may seem;
a state of mind where hope leaps up
at every passing footstep
in anticipation, wondering:
Could it be my love?

Perhaps the rule of love
may be no more certain of lasting
than the rule of fear—
but as to which one is worth having
while it lasts—
there is no uncertainty
as to that.

FOR HIMSELF

I like the myths about Zeus,
heaven's thunderbolted king,
having to come down from time to time
and take in his embrace
some mortal maiden,
timid, powerless, and innocent,
and entreat her to let him love her.
On these amatory adventures
the mighty god
usually took some simpler form—
swan or bull or mortal man.

Why should the god,
a handsome, bearded giant of a fellow,
have wanted to make
such a humble appearance?
Could it have been
that he had the same longing
all of us have,
and he wanted to be loved
for himself alone?

If he came as the god,
what mortal maiden would not love him,
or at least act as if she did—
out of the awe she felt for his power,
or the hope she felt for his favor,
or even because she felt,
by God, she'd better!

Could it be that he himself wanted to love,
not as the almighty king
doling out benevolence and charity

from his limitless, divine abundance,
but as the plain individual
feeling his own private heart expand
with the exquisite and intimate satisfaction
of loving someone
and being loved?
Not out of compassion,
but out of passion!

What if Almightiness
never felt love!
I wonder what kind of a world
a god who was without love
would have made—
not a world like this,
that's sure.
For all its agonies and imperfections,
it is not for lack of love
that this world suffers.

Whatever made this world,
it was not a God without feeling;
he may have had too much,
but not too little!
not the God who made me,
with my capacity for joy and pain
and love!

I believe if Almightiness
did not feel love,
it would destroy all it had made,
not to destroy us,
but in the hope it might
destroy itself.

I am glad when I read stories of God

wanting to love
and be loved,
not because he was God
but for himself.

IN ALL LOVE'S HOLY MOUNTAIN

Perhaps some day I will grow to the place
where I can live
by absolute love.
When I do this, will I find
absolute love
to be absolute power?

Will there be no need
to injure or kill
in all love's holy mountain?

When I have nothing left to give
and have given away
all I have to give,
holding nothing back
but letting go all
that was mine,
even myself,
then the whole universe,
abhorring a vacuum,
will rush to fill
the emptiness
that was myself
but is now only
my selflessness.

Thus, I shall become
the perfect vessel of love,
having nothing for myself
keeping nothing to myself
doing nothing by myself
being nothing in myself
but sharing all that is
with all that is.

This is to learn the deathless secret
of rivers and springs
and stars and the sun,
being filled
because you are empty,
being continually renewed
because you are perpetually consumed.

As for now,
I have no absolutes to live by.
The way I go is hardly ever clear
and every decision contains a thousand ifs.
Do I decree life and love?
I also decree death and pain.
The question is hardly ever either/or
but how much?
and for what?

NO RESISTANCE

When love offers no resistance,
does it become irresistible?

XVII.   The Miracle of Love

NO VOICE ANSWERED

Once there was a man in need of a revelation from God, for he was ill and in pain.

He had prayed for healing, but his prayers had not been answered. He had cried out for assurance, but he had heard no reassuring voice.

The man thought, "I have served God as well as I have been able. I have failed him, no doubt—perhaps in large ways, certainly in small ways—but I have served him. Why does he not help me?"

His wife helped him. He had merely to voice a request, and she ran to meet it. She even tried to foresee his needs and meet them before he asked. She kept watch by his bed day and night. He saw the look in his wife's eyes; it was a look of deep concern.

His friends helped him. They did his chores. They prayed for him. They sat by his bed and comforted him. He saw the look in his friends' eyes; it was a look of deep concern.

This was a man who had always had a deep sense of being unloved. But now the look in the eyes of his wife and friends was so much a look of love that he could not help realizing their love. He found himself saying, almost in astonishment, "These people love me."

Still, no miracle of healing happened when he prayed, and no voice answered when he called, "God, God!"

So the man continued to cry out in bitterness and doubt: "What kind of captain, hearing one of his company cry out in terror in the night, would not at least vouchsafe, 'Soldier, I am here. Take heart!'

"God, I ask no more than such a soldier. If you are there, let me know you are there."

Still, no voice spoke.

But the thought came to the man, "What do I mean when I say, 'God'?"

Then it occurred to him that he was asking for something to happen that he did not even believe in.

When he cried, "God!" he was looking not for God, but for a Thunderer. Yet he did not believe in a Thunderer. He was looking not for God, but for a kindly old man, like the Lord God Jehovah in *Green Pastures*. Yet he did not believe in a God like the one in *Green Pastures*.

Then the man stopped his crying, he stopped his complaining. He became still and asked himself, "What do I believe about God?"

It flashed into his mind that if someone asked him what he believed about God, he would have a hard time answering for the most part; but there was one thing he could say, had always said, and would say with certainty:

"God is love."

God is love!

Then he realized that all the time he had been crying and complaining, this God, the God who is love, had been revealing himself.

All the time he had been crying for God to appear, God had been appearing to him. He had been looking into the face of love. He had been looking into the only face love could show him, for it was the only face he had eyes to see. This was his wife's face. This was his friends' face.

All the time he had been crying out for God to speak, God had been speaking to him with the only voice the God of love could speak through, for it was the only voice he had ears to hear. This was his wife's voice. This was his friends' voice.

Then the man realized that all the time he had been begging for a revelation and a miracle, he had been receiving a revelation and a miracle. The name of the revelation is love. The name of the miracle is love.

WE CRY OUT, "GOD! GOD!"

Is there any higher revelation
or greater miracle
than love?

Sometimes miracles and revelations
are like flashes of lightning.
But sometimes they occur
so gradually and naturally
that we can hardly describe
what has occurred.
We can only say,
like the man born blind
whom Jesus healed:
"One thing I know,
that, whereas I was blind,
now I see."
We live in the midst
of a miracle.
Life is a miracle,
and presents us with
a succession of wonders.
These go on all the time;
they happen to us,
but we are not aware of them.
Then one day
we open our spiritual eyes
and exclaim,
"I see."

This man had thought
about God as love.
But he had never really considered what
God as love means.
Then one day

279

he opened his eyes
and saw
that God *is* love.
Suddenly God
was a real presence in his life,
in a way he had never been before.
God was no more
than God
had always been.
But the man
was aware of God,
not as a word,
not as an abstraction,
not as a distant being,
but as a present reality.
The man recognized God.

We are all much like this man.
We cry out,
"God! God!"
but we have not thought through
what we believe God to be.
We do not know what it is
we are expecting to see.

How can we hope to recognize him?

Would we feel our prayers were answered
if some sort of phantom presence
put in its appearance?
Or would we be terrified—
perhaps feel we were out of our mind?

IT IS YET MORE

When we cry, "God, God!"
we might be wise to think first
what it is that we expect.
What do we believe about God?

Certainly whatever made
the infinite universe,
whose scope and nature
we cannot imagine,
must be infinitely more than anything
we can imagine.
The supreme power
is not limited
by the limitations
of our thought about it.
Call it what name we will,
it is yet more.
The Chinese mystic Lao-tse said,
"The names that can be given
are not the Absolute Name."
Yet there are some things
we can say definitely
about the God
we believe in.
God must be good.
He must be infinitely better than we are,
than any man is.
He is good beyond
even our notions
of goodness.

THERE IS ONE NAME THAT IS WORTHY

Most of the names we call God
are not worthy of him.
They limit him.
They make him less than he is.
But there is one name
that is worthy
even of God.
This name is love.
For when we say
that God is love,
we are giving him
the highest, best, and most beautiful name there is
for that which is
highest, best, and most beautiful in this world.

God is love.

When we say that God is Allah,
we may separate ourselves
from all who are not Moslems.
When we say that God is Buddha,
we may separate ourselves
from all who are not Buddhists.
When we say that God is Christ,
we may separate ourselves
from all who are not Christians.
But when we say that God is love,
we make ourselves one
with all men,
and all men want to make themselves one
with us.

And God is God of all.
It is no virtue to address him in Latin

or Arabic or Sanskrit or English.
He is no respecter of persons
—or religions.
He is not available to one
and not to others.
God has no chosen people.
He has only people who have chosen God.
We choose him
not by repeating godly names
but by living godlike lives,
and a godlike life is above all
a life of love.

HE LIVED LOVE

Jesus came teaching faith,
but he also came teaching love.
This is what makes Jesus
supreme and unique.
He is love.

Other teachers have taught
detachment and withdrawal
as the way of life.
Jesus taught love.
He not only taught love.
He lived love.
He was incarnate selflessness.
He gave.
He forgave.
He healed.
He fed.
He comforted.
The sum of what he taught
and the sum of what he lived
is love.
"By this shall all men
know that ye are my disciples,"
he said at the Last Supper,
"if ye have love
one to another."
Not if you call yourself a Christian
—or a Baptist or a Catholic or a Unity student!
Not if you have secret knowledge
that no one else has!
Not if you live a life of austerity and denial!
Not if you are able to work miracles!
But "if ye have love one to another"!

"Love your enemies," he said.
"Pray for them who persecute you."
"Whosoever smiteth thee on thy right cheek,
turn to him the other also."
"Whosoever shall compel thee to go one mile,
go with him two."
"If any man would . . . take away thy coat,
let him have thy cloak also."

If these teachings seem impossible ideals,
it is only because
we have not love enough.
These are the words
of the Great Lover.
None but lovers
can follow this instruction.
When we love,
we do naturally
the things he told us to do.
We pray for those who persecute us
—when we love them.
We go the second mile,
we turn the other cheek
—for those we love.
We give our cloak
as well as our coat,
and everything else we own too,
when it is needed
—to those we love.
They don't have to ask us—
our wife or our grandson
or even our dog.
My dog got her paw stuck in the fence
and hung howling with pain.
When I tried to free her,
she bit me.
But I kept right on trying to set her free

even though she bit at me again,
and when I had her free,
I petted and comforted her
and calmed her fear.

Jesus loved.
As we love one or two,
he loved mankind.
For he knew that if we love,
we have the only life worth living.
To live for something more than ourself,
to live for others,
to live for God,
who is love
—this is the only life fit
for a son of man
and son of God.

FRIENDLY HANDS ARE EVERYWHERE

Sometimes we struggle to reach through to God
as if he were something
far away,
strange,
hard to find,
hard to understand.
Sometimes by the very urgency with which we seek him,
we separate ourselves
from him.
We are so intent on our search
that we pass him by.
We are looking far away,
and miss his beauty close at hand.
We are poring over strange matters
and fail to see his familiar truth.
We make him out to be a mysterious presence
—and waste our life looking for visions
and listening for voices.
We turn him into a vague abstraction
—and lose ourselves
in labyrinths of words.

And all the time
he is right here.
He is in us.
He is around us.
He is speaking to us with ten thousand tongues
and showing himself in ten thousand faces.
Looking for God
is like looking for the air
when all the time we are breathing it.
It is like looking for the sun
when all the time we are seeing,

walking, and living
by its light.

God is the love
in our own heart,
whatever love we may be capable of.
To find him,
we need go no further
than our own kind act
or charitable thought.

Once we have truly come to know God
as love,
we do not vainly call out,
"God! God!"
and agonize
for an answer.
We recognize him everywhere.

We see God looking at us
from the eyes of mothers and sweethearts,
wives and children,
neighbors and friends.
We see him in the eyes of strangers, too.
For they are love
as much as we are love.

When we know that God is love,
we feel his presence in the touch
of any friendly hand.
And we sense that friendly hands
are everywhere
—the hands of mothers,
the hands of teachers,
the hands of doctors,
the hands of ministers,
all the unseen hands

that do the many jobs
that make the human community
possible.

When we know that God is love,
we hear his voice in every cheerful word
that falls on our ears.
A glad "Good morning!"
becomes the speech of God.
The voice of God
is even the sound
of rain falling on the earth in spring.
In winter it is the silence
of the mantling snow.

When we know that God is love,
we never cease to hear his voice.
The silences declare his presence
as loudly as the thunder
or the sea.

When we know that God is love,
we truly find
sermons in stones
and God in everything.
The bread is love,
as it gives itself to us to be eaten.
The air is love,
as it gives itself to us to be breathed.
The sun is love,
as it gives us its light
that we may see.
In every loving thought, word, and act
we are one with him.

When we know that God is love,
we are never alone;

we never feel unloved.
We have made our abiding place
under the pinions of peace;
in the tower of the rock of the truth,
we have found our refuge.

Love casts out fear.
Love sets us free from self-concern.
Love soothes away pain.
Love is wholeness.

When we know that God is love,
we live in a friendly world.
For it is the world
that love has made.
And if we see pain
and unloveliness
that we cannot understand,
we feel no less
the infinite encompassing compassion
—over all a brooding
as of wings!
Nothing is without significance;
nothing is unimportant;
nothing will be left out.
In the likeness of love's loveliness,
all things have their true being.

Through all that is
—the moving spheres
and the lives of men
—we sense a harmony.
We are part of the harmony.
Knowing this, we have faith
to meet whatever we have to meet,
for we know that what we have to meet
is not meaningless and chance,

but also part of
the harmony.
Circumstance cannot separate us
from the calm assurance
of the working out of good.
We are in the care of that
which knows our need
better than we know it
and fills it before
we ask that it be filled.
We live under the shadow
of love.

NO STRANGER'S GUISE

O Child of Love,
why would you have God
be forever a strangeness and a mystery?
All the time he is knocking
at the door of your life,
and he has no stranger's guise.
He is the face of love
wherever it smiles at you.
He is the hand of love
wherever it is lifted to bless you.
He is the voice of love
wherever it rises in friendly greeting.

God cannot come to you in ways
that you cannot accept him,
but only in ways
that you can accept him.
How can he make himself more acceptable
than as love?
Would you have more of God?
Have more of love.
For God is love,
and love is God.
To have love in your heart
is to have God in your heart.
To have love in your heart
is to live in the heart of God.

TO END

Of all the hard things asked of human beings
nothing harder is asked
than that we love.
But once we love,
of all the hard things asked of human beings
nothing harder is asked
than that we
stop loving.